GEORGE WASHINGTON, NATIONALIST

GEORGE WASHINGTON, NATIONALIST

Edward J. Larson

UNIVERSITY OF VIRGINIA PRESS

Charlottesville and London

University of Virginia Press
© 2016 by the Rector and Visitors of the University of Virginia
All rights reserved
Printed in the United States of America on acid-free paper

First published 2016

1 3 5 7 9 8 6 4 2

Library of Congress Cataloging-in-Publication Data
Names: Larson, Edward J. (Edward John), author.
Title: George Washington, nationalist / Edward J. Larson.
Description: Charlottesville : University of Virginia Press, 2016. |
Series: Gay Hart Gaines distinguished lectures | Includes
bibliographical references and index.
Identifiers: LCCN 2016011407| ISBN 9780813938981 (cloth : alk. paper) |
ISBN 9780813938998 (e-book)
Subjects: LCSH: Washington, George, 1732-1799. | Washington,
George, 1732–1799—Influence. | United States—Politics and
government—1783–1789. | Nationalism—United States—History—
18th century. | Presidents—United States—Biography.
Classification: LCC E312.29 .L369 2016 | DDC 973.4/1092—dc23

LC record available at http://lccn.loc.gov/2016011407

FRONTISPIECE

*His Excel: G: Washington Esq: LLD. Late Commander in Chief
of the Armies of the U.S. of America & President of the
Convention of 1787,* by Charles Willson Peale, 1787.
(Used by permission of Mount Vernon Ladies' Association)

THE FRED W. SMITH
NATIONAL LIBRARY
FOR THE STUDY OF
GEORGE WASHINGTON
AT MOUNT VERNON

Preparation of this volume has been supported by The Fred W. Smith
National Library for the Study of George Washington at Mount Vernon
and by a gift from Mr. and Mrs. Lewis E. Lehrman.

Cover art: Washington on the dollar bill. (Shutterstock)

CONTENTS

THIS BOOK has a simple thesis. As one among many, George Washington was the leading nationalist of the late Revolutionary era in American history, a period lasting roughly from the British surrender at Yorktown in 1781 to the first federal election in 1789. This does not mean that Washington was a political philosopher. For a political philosopher of nationalism from that period in America, one would need to look to James Madison, Alexander Hamilton, or John Jay—though even that might stretch the term. This was a period of political action more than philosophical reflection. And Washington was a man of inspired action rather than deep thought. As a result, this book chronicles his actions during this critical period more than it analyzes his ideas. From those actions, however, a concerted pattern emerges that led toward the forming of a lasting and more perfect union of the thirteen American states. It is that story this book seeks to tell.

Each book springs from many sources; every author owes heavy debts. These facts are especially apparent in this instance. The text is adapted and enlarged from the three lectures I gave as part of the Gay Hart Gaines Lecture Series at Mount Vernon in the fall of 2014. Those lectures in turn were adapted from my book *The Return of George Washington, 1783–1789*. And that 2014 book benefited from resources used and relationships developed during my tenure as an Inaugural Fellow at the Fred W. Smith National Library for the Study of George Washington at Mount Vernon. This background creates at least three distinct levels of sources and debts for the current work.

First, without the support and stimulus of the Gaines Lecture Series, and the relationship between that Mount Vernon series and the University of Virginia Press, this book would not exist. My basic work on George Washington done, I would have turned to other topics. That lecture series forced me to develop ideas explored in my earlier work and respond to issues raised during my presentations. And the resulting opportunity to publish this second book both allowed and obligated me to pursue these ideas and issues. My thanks go to the Mount Vernon Ladies' Association, particularly Regent Barbara Lucas and Vice Regent for Wisconsin Anne Petri, Association President Curt Viebranz, University of Virginia Press History and Social Sciences Editor Dick Holway, and the former vice regent for whom the lecture series is named, Gay Hart Gaines. I also drew on other lectures I was invited to give following the publication of my earlier book, including one delivered near the Revolutionary War encampment at Newburgh, New York, and another on presidential leadership given in honor and memory of my Williams College political science professor James MacGregor Burns.

Second, without my earlier book, *The Return of George Washington,* there would not have been this second one. I owe a compound debt to the people and institutions that assisted me in researching, writing, and publishing that book, many of which are noted in its preface. My editor for *The Return of George Washington,* Peter Hubbard, merits my special thanks both for his assistance with that book and for extending the permission of its publisher, the William Morrow imprint of HarperCollins, for the University of Virginia Press to publish this one. Although largely limited to the same period of Washington's life, 1783–89, the current work is more than a derivative product of the earlier one. New themes are explored, and added sources are exploited. The focus shifts and narrows to nationalism. Still, much is borrowed, recycled, and reused. *The Return of George Washington* remains the broader study, more fully narrating Washington's life from his retirement as commander-in-chief of American forces during the Revolutionary War in 1783 to his inauguration as the first president of the United States under the Constitution in 1789. Even after reading this focused study of Washington's nationalism during this critical period, I urge those interested in the full narrative to consult that earlier work. There is more there than here, just as there is some here that is not there.

Finally, I wish to acknowledge the support provided by the staff of the Fred W. Smith National Library for the Study of George Washington — particularly the founding director, Doug Bradburn; the manager of library services, Stephen McLoud; the historian, Mary Thompson; and the photograph archivist, Dawn Bonner — during my fellowship at Mount Vernon in 2013 and beyond. Not only did their help with my research on that earlier occasion directly aid me in preparing the current manuscript but they extended further assistance beyond the scope of my original fellowship as I composed and revised it. My special thanks go to Peter R. Henriques, a distinguished Washington scholar and emeritus professor of history at George Mason University, who generously reviewed my manuscript twice and offered all manner of invaluable suggestions, and to Rick Britton for his expert assistance with two new maps for this volume.

The preface to my first book on Washington begins and ends by describing the inspiration provided by residing and working at Mount Vernon. To a historian of the Revolutionary era, the place is magical and its resources invaluable. Writing this second book allowed me to spend a few added days and nights there. More sunrises over the Potomac River and dusks settling over the fields behind the main house extended the spell cast

by my original residency. For that, this book is better than it
otherwise would have been.

Prefaces are composed last. This one is written at Mount
Vernon on a late-summer afternoon near a tulip poplar tree
planted by the General in 1785, during the period covered by
this book. With deep roots and towering crown, that tree ex-
tends a welcome shadow for those passing by on hot, sunny
days. Shortly before planting that tree, Washington wrote to
his wartime colleague the Chevalier de Chastellux about the
gratitude he received from the shade of trees he had planted at
Mount Vernon in his youth. Reflecting on this comment in the
shade of his tulip poplar, I think of the gratitude Americans
owe Washington for the enduring influence of the services he
performed and precedents he set in helping to forge the nation.
Those services and precedents still cast a welcome shadow.

CHAPTER ONE

Planning for Peace

1783

IN THE SPRING OF 1783, with the American Revolution drawing to a close, George Washington faced a critical decision, and he would face several more over the next six years. Nurtured in the Enlightenment values of elite Virginian society during the mid-eighteenth century, Washington believed in the Lockean natural rights of free men and the republican ideals of government by the consent of the governed.

Taking those values to heart, he had joined the patriot cause eight years earlier and, already known for his service as a colonel in the Virginia militia during the colonial French and Indian War, had been elected by the Continental Congress to lead the troops fighting first against British oppression and, after July 1776, for American independence. Those troops ultimately combined the militias of many states with continental units into a force that ranged freely across traditional colonial boundaries from Massachusetts to Georgia, with Washington personally directing major battles in five different states and commanding men from all thirteen.

This experience gave Washington a continental vision and a national perspective. No longer merely a colonial Virginian in outlook, with the war ending he would return his military commission to Congress and resume his prewar life as a Tidewater planter. But he could never really be the same person again. He could not lay down his nationalism as easily as he had his sword.

During eight years of war Washington repeatedly denied having any personal ambitions of his own in the fight for American independence. He served without pay or leave throughout the period and repeatedly vowed to retire at the war's end. Indeed, reflecting his republican ideals, just ten days after his appointment in 1775 Washington famously declared that by becoming a soldier he "did not lay aside the Citizen."[1] It was his way of affirming civilian rule and renouncing military pretensions. Yet, as the war wound down following the victory of combined state, continental, and French forces under Washington over British troops at the Siege of Yorktown in 1781, the decision to step down as commander-in-chief and leave political power in the hands of thirteen sovereign states and their Confederation Congress might not have seemed as simple as it had in the heady days of the war's outset.

The war itself had not gone as smoothly as either side had initially expected, and Washington had suffered a long learning curve as commander-in-chief. After winning public acclaim for successfully forcing the British to evacuate Boston in March 1776 without much loss of life on either side, Washington faced near disaster five months later when the British returned with overwhelming force to reclaim their colonies. Beginning with the Battle of Long Island in August, they routed Washington's army in a series of clashes that had driven the Americans across the Delaware River and into Pennsylvania by the end of November. Seeking to consolidate their gains in New York and New Jersey, the British then settled in for the winter with the expectation of finishing off the rebels in the spring. Leading what was left of his beleaguered army back across the Delaware on Christmas night, however, Washington captured the advance British outpost at Trenton. The British viewed this setback as minor, but patriot propagandists made the most of it. Despite a disastrous summer, Washington grew in stature.

The summer of 1777 went much like the summer of 1776 for Washington, with the British pushing his army back through New Jersey and deep into Pennsylvania. In October, however, at the Second Battle of Saratoga, a separate American force under General Horatio Gates captured a British army invading from Canada, leading France to join the war on the patriot side a year later. The British responded by massing their northern troops in easily defended Manhattan and sending a second army south by ship to roll up the southern colonies, which they viewed as more valuable and loyal to Britain than the northern ones. For the next three years, Washington countered by keeping his main force in and around New York to contain the British there and relying mostly on southerners to defend themselves. Initially at least, the British strategy worked. After Savannah and Charleston fell, a British army under Lord Cornwallis pushed north into Virginia in 1781. Washington then took the risk of shifting his main army to Virginia, where with the aid of a French fleet it captured Cornwallis's army at Yorktown, all but compelling Britain to accept American independence. Returning with his men to the lower Hudson River valley around Newburgh, New York, he guarded against an outbreak by the remaining British forces in Manhattan for nearly two years while American peace negotiators in Paris struggled to resolve the war on favorable terms.

Despite the decisive victory at Yorktown, problems persisted for the American union. Indeed, in some respects they worsened. Having not yet entered into a peace treaty, Britain continued to hamstring American trade on the high seas and to occupy three key American ports: New York, Charleston, and Savannah. Economic conditions deteriorated in many places. The end of British offensive operations on land, however, by reducing the sense of crisis at home, weakened the resolve of states to work together. Each increasingly went its own way in addressing domestic political and economic issues even at the expense of other states; none showed much concern for the central union, and many reduced their support for the Continental army. This worried Washington.

The United States then operated under the Articles of Confederation, which created a league of thirteen sovereign states. Although they created a Congress with authority over foreign affairs and the war effort, and Americans at the time viewed their revolt as a single combined effort rather than coordinated rebellions by thirteen separate states, the Articles reserved to the states the power to levy taxes, to appoint military officers below the rank of general, and to regulate commerce. To pay soldiers, purchase supplies, and perform other necessary functions, Congress relied on voluntary requisitions from the states coupled with foreign and domestic loans. Neither source, nor both together, brought in enough cash to cover expenses. Any enforceable national tax required ratification by all thirteen states, which never happened. Further, Congress itself operated at the whim of the states. Its members were chosen by the various state legislatures rather than by voters, recallable at will, and paid by their respective states. Each state, from tiny Delaware to massive Virginia with ten times as many free people (thirteen times more if one includes slaves), had but one vote, which was exercisable by a majority of its members present and subject to instruction by the state. Given its weakness, by the 1780s Congress rarely had a quorum of states present, and all thirteen were never represented at the same time.

Without taxing authority, Congress defaulted on some of its debts and all but stopped paying the troops. Fearing they would never be repaid, an increasing number of domestic lenders sold their government bonds to speculators—sometimes for pennies on the dollar—creating a new class of government creditors whom many citizens did not feel morally obliged to compensate. Further, in 1779, as the war wore on with no end in sight, the Continental Congress promised army officers, in return for remaining in the service, a postwar pension of half pay for seven years — and extended it to half pay for life a year later — creating another unfunded government obligation that many Americans opposed. These elite army pensioners would create a privileged class at taxpayer expense, critics complained.

These unpopular debts gave added excuses for cash-strapped states to cut their payments to Congress, which was on the verge of bankruptcy by the end of 1782. While war had served as a main reason for the states to cooperate, its impending end threatened to further undermine their support for Congress. Soldiers and creditors alike worried that once peace came, they would never be paid. This desperate fiscal situation created a combustible environment at Newburgh that was destined to test Washington's republican ideas.

WITH WASHINGTON'S tacit approval, during the closing days of 1782 a delegation of officers from the Newburgh encampment led by Major General Alexander McDougall carried a petition to Congress, which then met in Philadelphia. Signed by Washington's loyal second-in-command, Henry Knox, the petition appealed for the ascertainment of the amount owed each officer for back pay and expenses, with security established for timely payment. It also contained an offer to accept lump-sum payments in lieu of the officers' unpopular half-pay pensions. Reading like the work of a committee, the petition awkwardly lurched from poignant first-person laments through objective-sounding accounts of the army's neglect by Congress to a thinly veiled third-person threat. "We have borne all that men can bear," the petitioners grumbled, "our property is expended, our private resources are at an end, and our friends are wearied out and disgusted with our incessant applications." Whether because of

Congress's want of means or failure of supply, the petition observed, troops had suffered all manner of scarcity and shortage throughout the war. "The uneasiness of the soldiers, for want of pay, is great and dangerous," it warned at one key point. "Any further experiment on their patience may have fatal effects."[2]

Upon its arrival, McDougall's delegation was embraced by Congress's superintendent of finance, Robert Morris, who managed the government's business operations with an iron fist. A cunning and wealthy Philadelphia merchant, Morris had championed the cause of a strong central government for so long and with such ardor that he had split Congress into pro-Morris and anti-Morris camps. During the mid-1780s these would evolve into recognizable nationalist and antinationalist factions, with the former favoring a strong central government within a federal system and the latter preferring a weak confederation of sovereign states. His tireless efforts to supply the troops during the war had made Morris a close ally of Washington, who ultimately emerged as the public face of nationalism.

Adding to the warmth of their welcome by some, the officers from Newburgh reached Philadelphia only days after Morris learned that the states had failed to ratify his proposal for a national tax, or "impost," on all goods coming from overseas, which he had pushed through Congress as the means to pay past debts and finance ongoing operations. Nationalists in Congress saw the officers' petition as a timely tool to revive the impost. All they needed to gain its ratification, some overly optimistic nationalists believed, was for the army to link its worthy cause and veiled threats with the creditors' political clout and Congress's proposed solution.[3] More cynical nationalists privately conceded that it might take an actual show of force by the unpaid troops to secure taxing authority for Congress from the states. And there was no greater cynic among the nationalists than Robert Morris's wise and worldly assistant, Gouverneur Morris, who on New Year's Day 1783 wrote a cryptic note to the American peace negotiator John Jay in Paris about soldiers "with swords in their hands" securing that power for Congress "without which the government is but a name." He promised Jay, "Depend on it, good will arise from the situation to which we are hastening."[4]

Historians have long debated exactly which situation Morris had in mind—mere threats or actual insurrection—and how much the two Morrises and Washington's former aide New York congressman Alexander Hamilton tried to hasten it. Certainly, they were wily politicians who fought fiercely for their ends and at the time viewed the taxing power as an essential end for stable government. After conferring with them, McDougall's delegation began warning Congress that the troops might mutiny without pay. On January 9, 1783, McDougall wrote to Knox about the benefits of uniting "the influence of Congress with that of the Army and the public creditors to obtain permanent funds for the United States."[5] Here lay the conspiracy with the army at its heart.

In early February, after neither Congress nor the army took the bait, McDougall and Gouverneur Morris wrote to Knox reiterating the government's dire fiscal situation and urging the army to join with other public creditors in pressuring the states to ratify the impost.[6] Word of a peace treaty with Britain might come at any moment and undermine the army's leverage, they warned. With peace, Congress could simply send the troops home without paying them. Writing under the ominous pseudonym Brutus, McDougall separately advised Knox that the army might refuse to disband until the troops were paid and pensions funded. Any message to Knox would surely reach Washington. Mutiny was in the air.

Despite these provocations, Knox remained silent, and Newburgh quiet, until mid-February, when word reached America that the British government had agreed to independence. Going over Knox's head, Hamilton wrote directly to Washington warning him of rumors that to secure what was due them and maybe more, some unpaid officers at Newburgh might reject his leadership and use the army to secure their pay and pension.[7] Hamilton's letter could be read as urging Washington either to channel the insurrection in ways that would strengthen the central government at the expense of the states or to squelch it in advance. Hoping that either option might ultimately aid the nationalist cause, Hamilton probably intended both readings and left it to Washington to choose.[8]

Washington chose the latter option for himself, the army, and his country. Responding to Hamilton, Washington blamed the dissension in camp on General Horatio Gates — "the old le[a]ven," he called him — and junior officers at Gates's headquarters near Newburgh. Despite this mutinous faction and the injustices suffered by all, under his "steady" leadership "the sensible, and the discerning part of the Army" would remain loyal, Washington assured Hamilton. Reminded of his support and sacrifice, Washington wrote, the officers and their men would follow him into peaceful retirement even though "the prevailing sentiment in the Army is that the prospect of compensation for past services will terminate with the war."[9]

Some officers were already falling into line. On February 21, presumably at Washington's request, Knox had finally replied to McDougall's conspiratorial missives. In his letter Knox had distanced himself and Washington's army from any effort to use soldiers for domestic political purposes. "I consider the reputation of the American Army as one of the most immaculate things on earth," he wrote in words that captured Washington's views as well as his own. "We should even suffer wrongs and injury to the utmost verge of toleration rather than sully it in the least degree."[10] Despite Knox's willingness to raise issues of dissension in the ranks as part of the officers' petition for back pay, he would not brook strong-arm tactics or active disobedience to civilian authority. Washington felt similarly.

Notwithstanding these confident words from Washington and Knox, mutinous rumblings among junior officers at Gates's headquarters agitated the encampment. With a nod from the General or perhaps even by his looking away, following word in mid-March of a preliminary peace with Britain those rumblings threatened to erupt into an army-wide revolt against civilian rule. At the time, Washington attributed this development to the arrival from Philadelphia of a former Gates aide, Walter Stewart, with promises of support from other government creditors and aid from nationalists in Congress should the army rise up and demand justice.[11] The cabal may have included Gates and the Morrises.[12] Hamilton almost certainly knew about it; some historians surmise that he orchestrated it.[13]

On March 10 the conspirators at Newburgh distributed an anonymous call for a general meeting of field officers and company representatives on the following day along with an unsigned address outlining their demands. Congress had promised to pay the troops, the address began, "but faith has its limits, as well as temper; and there are points beyond which neither can be stretched, without sinking into cowardice, or plunging into credulity." The meek language of the officers' petition had produced nothing, the writer noted. "If this, then, be your treatment while the swords you wear are necessary for the defense of America, what have you to expect from peace?" To avoid "poverty, wretchedness, and contempt" in old age, the address called on officers to "suspect the man who would advise to more moderation" — presumably Washington — and present members of Congress with a stark alternative. If peace came without payment, officers should tell them that "nothing shall separate them from your arms but death"; if war continued, they should "retire to some unsettled country, smile in your turn, and 'mock when their fear cometh on.'"[14] The treasonous blast was written by one of Gates's junior officers, Major John Armstrong, and copied by another, Captain Christopher Richmond.

Washington reacted swiftly. He issued general orders disallowing the anonymously called meeting. Perhaps fearing that it might proceed anyway in the absence of an orderly alternative, however, he authorized a similar meeting for March 15 and directed Gates to preside.[15] The orders suggested that Washington would not attend. Perhaps, some suggested, the General was giving his tacit support. In a second unsigned address written by Armstrong, the conspirators accepted the later meeting date. Assembling under Washington's authority would add force to any resulting resolutions, the second address noted, without lessening the officers' "independency" of action.[16] The conspirators' mutinous demands remained the sole item on the meeting's agenda. The camp buzzed in anticipation. Officers from every unit in the Newburgh encampment attended the meeting, perhaps five hundred in all. They had little else to do and much pent-up frustration. As soon as Gates called the session to order, Washington dramatically and unexpectedly strode into the encampment's makeshift wooden meeting hall, known as the Temple, and asked to speak first.

As was his custom on formal occasions, Washington read a prepared statement. He had drafted it himself. It was "the most impressive speech he ever wrote," the historian Joseph Ellis later observed.[17] Less than two thousand words long, it spoke of his sacrifices, a soldier's duty, and the impracticability of the conspirators' scheme. To secure the officers' back pay and future pensions, Washington vowed to do as much "as may be done consistently with the great duty I owe to my country." That duty, he implied, demanded deference to civilian authority, with all legitimate governing authority deriving from the consent of the governed and never from the force of arms, no matter how justified. And nothing mattered more to Washington than duty, and honor. So he admonished his officers, "As you value your own sacred honor," to "express your utmost horror and detestation of the Man who wishes, under any specious pretences, to overturn the liberties of our Country, and who wickedly attempts to open the flood Gates of Civil discord, and deluge our rising Empire in Blood."[18] "Our *empire*," he called it. Not "our *states*," not even "our *republic*," whatever that might have meant at the time, but a single empire composed of thirteen states much as any empire then or before united distinct political units under one supreme governing authority. This was his American empire, a nation of states.

After concluding his short but stern speech, Washington reached into his coat pocket for a letter from a friendly congressman, Virginia's Joseph Jones. It reiterated the extreme gravity of the government's financial situation and summarized the ongoing efforts of Congress to address it. At some point, either while reading his speech or while reading this letter—contemporary accounts differ about the timing—Washington drew reading glasses from his waistcoat and asked, "Gentleman, you will permit me to put on my spectacles, for I have not only grown gray but almost blind in the service of my country."[19] Few of the officers had seen Washington wear glasses. Coming in conjunction with his hard address, this soft show of familiarity in their presence moved many. It both humanized and elevated him. Whether because of his lofty words or because of his lowly gesture, some officers wept openly. With this finely timed performance Washington carried the day. After he left, the officers quickly approved resolutions prepared in advance by Knox asking Washington to represent their interests before Congress and repudiating both the "infamous propositions" contained in the two unsigned addresses and the conspirators behind them.[20] Fifty years later, testifying to its significance in their eyes, survivors of the episode joined a later generation of Americans in erecting on the site an obelisk bearing the words "Birthplace of the Republic," for here, they believed, the United States as a single nation under republican rule had been born. Washington had not created it any more than he had won the Revolutionary War, but he had given it voice at Newburgh and through his officers' responses helped to make it a reality.

In 1783, as word of the encounter first reached Congress and then spread across the land in newspaper accounts, Washington gained yet another laurel. Already first in war, he was now first in peace and clearly first in the hearts of his countrymen. He had no rivals. As their own financial situation went from bad to worse, however, many of the unpaid officers soon regretted their decision to follow Washington and trust Congress. When most of them were furloughed that summer in anticipation of peace, their bitterness had grown so great that a planned farewell banquet with Washington was canceled. All of those involved feared that the event might turn sour. Even Washington began to doubt the course he had recommended for his men, at least to the extent that it relied on trusting in the goodwill of Congress. By this time, though, the twig was bent, and so it grew. Taking to heart his vow to champion the officers' cause, Washington began to use his platform as America's leading citizen to call for quickly and fairly compensating the troops, and ultimately for building a strong national union that could support those payments and some form of permanent military establishment. Indeed, one could say that the long road to constitutional reform that culminated five years later in a new federal system began in Newburgh with Washington's commitment to fair treatment for his officers and soldiers.

HAMILTON AND THE Newburgh Conspiracy may have helped to force the cautious Virginian's hand on the thorny issues of national sovereignty and constitutional reform, but Washington played it with conviction. Because of the formal cessation of hostilities in April 1783 and the pending furlough of most soldiers and officers over the ensuing summer, the commander-in-chief had time to focus on the country's future as he waited with a skeleton force for the final peace treaty and the departure of the last British troops from New York. The process dragged on until November. Early in that prolonged period of enforced inactivity, Washington issued the two most significant documents of his military career. Though both took years to bear fruit, they helped to lay a foundation for the new constitutional order that Washington would eventually lead.

The first, "Sentiments on a Peace Establishment," drew on the work of various staff and field officers but carried Washington's personal and official stamp. It ran counter to conventional wisdom. During the conflict, few Americans had thought realistically about the postwar military. Oppressed by professional British and paid Hessian soldiers before and during the Revolutionary War, and hesitant to assume the cost of a peacetime military, most Americans instinctively opposed a standing army. State and local militias had risen to the defense of individual liberty against imperial troops and presumably would melt away with peace.

Monarchies needed a professional army to gain and retain power, many Americans thought, but not republics. As a people, however, they lacked reference points. In the popular mind, the only successful republican governments were ancient Greek city-states and modern Swiss cantons. These tiny islands of popular rule, so far as Americans knew, had been or were defended by citizen soldiers. Republican Rome, once it gained size, had fallen to its own power-hungry military leaders. In his "Sentiments," Washington began changing the conversation at least insofar as it related to the needs of a continental republic with international commercial interests and imperial ambitions of its own on the western frontier.

"Altho' a large standing Army in time of Peace hath ever been considered dangerous to the liberties of a Country, yet a few Troops, under certain circumstances, are not only safe, but indispensably necessary," Washington began. These would be "Continental Troops" of the national government, he stressed, organized into four regiments of infantry and one of artillery to secure the western frontier and guard the border with Brit-ish Canada. Existing state militias would be restructured on a Swiss model as a uniform force of citizen soldiers ready for call-up in times of need and, once called, under central com-mand. Washington also urged that the national government build coastal fortifications and a navy to protect commerce, maintain a base at West Point to block invasion from Canada, and open an academy to train army officers. But his main con-cern was the West, notably the old Northwest, where Virgin-ians were settling and where he had investments. States were in the process of ceding their western land claims to the central government, and many people saw the West as key to the coun-try's future. Washington called for creating a series of military posts up the Potomac valley, along the Ohio River, north to the Great Lakes, and west to the Mississippi. "The Tribes of Indians within our Territory are numerous, soured and jeal-ous," he warned.[21] If accepted, Washington's proposal would go a long way toward forging a continental union and giving it national purpose.

Of far greater import, Washington followed this proposal, which he submitted to Congress, with a circular letter to the thirteen state governments. An appeal for unity at a time when peace with Britain had removed the common enemy that had drawn the states together, the letter built to its main point: national sovereignty. "It is indispensable to the happiness of the individual States, that there should be lodged somewhere, a Supreme Power to regulate and govern the general concerns of the Confederated Republic." Long on theme but short on specifics, the letter called for "entire conformity to the Spirit of the Union," a continental army supported by uniform state militias, taxing power for Congress, and "complete justice to all the Public Creditors," particularly the unpaid troops. Its pounding theme throughout—from Washington's opening appeal to "citizens of America" through his depiction of "the glorious Fabrick of our . . . National Character" to his closing prayer for "a happy Nation"—was American nationhood. "It is only in our united Character as an Empire, that our Independence is acknowledged," Washington reminded his readers. Split apart, the states would be reabsorbed by Britain one by one, he warned. And if, blessed with "a fairer opportunity for political happiness than any other nation has ever been favored with" and after the sacrifice of "so much blood and treasure," America lost its bold experiment with liberty, it would be the fault of the citizenry.[22]

Arguably the most lyrical and impactful composition of his life, the 1783 Circular to the States set forth four "pillars" that Washington depicted as essential for national well-being, happiness, and independence. First, he called for "An indissoluble Union of the States under one Federal Head." Once in, never out. No revolving-door confederacy but an eternal union founded on liberty. Anything less, Washington warned, would tend toward anarchy and confusion. "Whoever would dare to sap the foundation, or overturn the Structure," he wrote, "will merit the bitterest execration, and the severest punishment which can be inflicted." Second, appealing in part for his unpaid troops but also reflecting a broad vision for the rule of law, Washington urged "a Sacred regard to Public Justice," without which liberty would be lost. Third, based on his wartime experience and on his belief that a strong military under civilian control was necessary for peace, he advocated "the adoption of a proper Peace Establishment" along the lines of the proposal he had already sent to Congress. Finally, Washington called on all "the People of the United States" to adopt a disposition toward one another "which will induce them to forget their local prejudices and policies, to make those mutual concessions which are requisite to the general prosperity, and in some instances, to sacrifice their individual advantages to the interest of the Community." This, he held, was the essence of citizenship.[23]

In opening and closing the letter, Washington played his trump card. His words on this matter could be trusted, he wrote, because he was relinquishing power soon and "not taking any share in public business hereafter." For the first time in a public statement, he declared his firm intent to retire. Not seeking power for himself, Washington observed, he could have no "sinister views" in promoting a strong national government. At the time, Washington viewed the circular letter as something of a farewell to the American people and asked that they accept it as "the Legacy of One, who has ardently wished, on all occasions, to be useful to his Country."[24] Certainly Americans received it as such. Hailed as "Washington's Legacy," the letter appeared in newspapers from New England to the Deep South and became one of the most celebrated documents of the day.[25] Though none of its nation-building recommendations were realized for more than five years, they immediately became associated with Washington. Indeed, in the public imagination that Virginian had become the first American.

THE CIRCULAR LETTER to the states thus set the stage for what Washington said and many believed would be his concluding acts as a public official. They began in Newburgh on November 2, after news of the final peace treaty reached New York, when the General sent his farewell orders to his soldiers, whom he affectionately addressed as "one patriotic band of Brothers." They should return home as citizens of the United States, he urged, not as people of the various states.[26] Many had already left; most soon followed. This admonishment of citizenship, though timely and appropriate coming from their commander-in-chief to the departing men, was less an order than a reminder, because the nationalistic urge had emanated from below as well as from above. Washington assimilated it from his men, particular such close aides as Knox of Massachusetts, the Caribbean-born and New York–educated Hamilton, South Carolina's John Laurens, and the Pennsylvanian Joseph Reed, as much as they assimilated it from him. As a fraternal band, the officers and soldiers had fought together across state boundaries for a common cause: American independence. This was the sentiment Washington hoped they would take home to their states. It was typically not as strong among those like Patrick Henry, who did not serve in a national capacity during the war.

After triumphantly leading the residual Continental troops and assembled New York militia into a war-scarred Manhattan after the British finally evacuated it on November 30, a second farewell occurred when Washington attended a midday banquet with his remaining officers at Fraunces Tavern, near the dock where a barge waited to ferry him to New Jersey on his way home. After everyone had a glass of wine, Washington raised his in a hand quivering from sentiment. "With an heart full of love and gratitude, I now take leave of you," he said in a toast. "I must devoutly wish that your latter days may be as prosperous and happy, as your former ones have been glorious and honourable."[27] Choked with emotion, Washington could not say more; nor could anyone else. After embracing each man, he left on a two-week celebratory journey through New Jersey, Pennsylvania, and Delaware to Annapolis, Maryland, where Congress then met to escape the unrest caused by unpaid troops in Philadelphia, the government's customary seat. At every stop, Washington reminded the assembled dignitaries and cheering townspeople of the need to strengthen the central government, a theme he repeated in Annapolis. There, after four days of public celebration, in a final farewell, Washington formally resigned his commission as commander-in-chief.

Following a script prepared by a congressional committee chaired by Thomas Jefferson, Washington entered the Assembly Chamber in Annapolis at noon on December 23, 1783, and took a seat opposite the seated president of Congress, Thomas Mifflin. The other members of Congress also sat, and all wore hats. The French ambassador, Maryland state officials, and leading citizens of Annapolis then entered the hall—men standing at the rear, women in the gallery above. Once the spectators had settled in their places, Mifflin addressed the General, "Sir, The U.S. in Congress Assembled are prepared to receive your Communications."[28] Washington rose and bowed to Congress. On this cue, the members doffed their hats but did not stand. This stiff protocol maintained that the members of Congress were respectfully superior to the commander-in-chief. Drawing a paper written in his own hand from a coat pocket, Washington then read his final address as a military commander. Scarcely three hundred words long, it made history.

"The great events on which my resignation depended, having at length taken place," Washington began, his hand trembling, revealing his emotion, "I have now the honor of offering my sincere Congratulations to Congress, and of presenting myself before them, to surrender into their hands the trust committed to me." Soon he needed both hands to steady the page. After noting the "diffidence" with which he had initially accepted the post, acknowledging his "obligations" to the army in general and his closest aides in particular, and "commending the interests of our dearest country to the protection of Almighty God," Washington concluded, "I retire from the great theatre of action, and bidding an affectionate farewell to this august body, under whose orders I have so long acted, I here offer my commission, and take my leave of all the employments of public life."[29] By this point all the spectators were weeping, one observer noted, "and there was hardly a member of Congress who did not drop tears."[30] Drawing his commission from his coat pocket, Washington then stepped forward and handed it to the president.

A future American government chose to memorialize this precise moment in one of eight historical paintings decorating the rotunda of the United States Capitol. Turned slightly to the right toward Congress, Washington dominates the image at the center, framed by a broad pilaster added to the background by the artist John Trumbull to convey stability. His left hand on a riding whip to suggest the haste with which he rode to Congress to relinquish power, Washington reaches out his right hand, with the commission, toward Mifflin, who stands on a raised platform, slightly higher than the General, to show civilian authority but is still smaller than Washington and painted in flat profile within a formal group portrait of all twenty congressmen. To depict the four future Virginia presidents as united for this foundational episode, Jefferson, James Madison, and James Monroe are identifiable in this stylized grouping even though Madison had not rejoined Congress following its remove to Annapolis. Behind Washington on his left stand an equal number of spectators, with his wife Martha,

General George Washington Resigning His Commission,
by John Trumbull, 1824.
(Used by permission of Architect of the Capitol)

who was not actually there, gazing down from the gallery in domestic garb.

The tableau unfrozen in real time, President Mifflin then stiffly read the elegant response that Jefferson's committee had drafted for the occasion. "The U.S. in congress assembled receive with emotions too affecting for utterance this solemn Resignation of the authorities under which you have led their troops with Success through a perilous and doubtful war," it began in soaring words that surely came from Jefferson, who had penned the lofty Declaration of Independence eight long years before. "Having defended the standard of liberty in this new world . . . you retire from the great theatre of action with the blessings of your fellow citizens, but the glory of your virtues will not terminate with your military command, it will continue to animate remotest ages."[31] Observing that Washington had accepted his post when the lack of foreign alliances and a central government made the war's outcome doubtful, the response now hailed the commander-in-chief's military leadership and deference to civilian authority. It concluded with a prayer to God for Washington that "a life so beloved may be fostered with all his care; that your days may be happy as they have been illustrious; and that he will finally give you that reward which this world cannot give."[32] His resignation duly accepted, Washington bowed again to Congress and was free to go. He stayed only long enough to greet the members following their adjournment and was riding toward his Mount Vernon plantation by two o'clock. He had promised Martha that he would be home for Christmas. He kept his word.

Extolled by later historians as a signal event that set the country's political course—Thomas Fleming called it "the most important moment in American history"[33]—Washington's retirement was similarly praised at the time. Citing examples from Julius Caesar to Oliver Cromwell, British leaders during the war had scoffed at Americans for rebelling against one King George only to gain another in George Washington. Successful rebel leaders inevitably became tyrants, they had charged. Indeed, in England, when the expatriate American painter Benjamin West predicted that Washington would retire upon the cessation of hostilities, a skeptical King George III reportedly replied, "If he does that, he will be the greatest man in the world."[34] Writing from London after word of Washington's resignation reached that city, West's American student John Trumbull wrote to his brother in Connecticut that the act "excites the astonishment and admiration of this part of the world. 'Tis a Conduct so novel, so inconceivable to People, who, far from giving up powers they possess, are willing to convulse the Empire to acquire more."[35] No wonder Trumbull later painted the scene with such feeling.

In America, Washington at once became a second Cincinnatus, the legendary ancient leader twice called from his farm and given supreme power to rescue republican Rome from its enemies only to relinquish power and return to his farm once the dangers had passed. A firsthand account from Annapolis printed in countless American newspapers during January 1784 described the event as "extraordinary, and to the General more honourable than any that is recorded in history."[36] A member of Congress from Maryland and a future secretary of war, James McHenry, writing to his fiancée on the twenty-third, spoke of it as "a solemn and affecting spectacle; such an one as history does not present."[37]

After reflecting for three months on what had transpired, Jefferson commented, "The moderation and virtue of a single character probably prevented this revolution from being closed, as most others have been by a subversion of that liberty it was intended to establish."[38] Even more than the commander-in-chief's distinguished and disinterested service during the Revolutionary War, which was performed without salary or leave for more than eight and one-half years, voluntarily surrendering the trappings of power for private life on a Virginia plantation made Washington a venerated American hero and a world-renowned personification of republican virtue.

CHAPTER TWO

Empire Rising in the West

1784–1785

RETIREMENT? Today, Americans often think of retirement as golf, bridge, and a condo in Florida or Arizona with no grass to mow, but what would it mean to George Washington? He used the word often in 1783 as the Revolutionary War was winding down and he prepared to resign his commission as commander-in-chief of American forces in December. Mount Vernon would be the "seat of my retirement from the bustle of the busy world," Washington wrote in one typical letter.[1] Yet what did Washington envision as retirement? He was only fifty-one years old and the most celebrated person in America, the master of one of Virginia's largest plantations, and justly proud of and profoundly concerned about his country and his reputation. If by *to retire* one means "to rest," Washington knew that would not be the case.

First, he had plenty to do on his Mount Vernon plantation. "An almost entire suspension of every thing which related to my own Estate, for near nine years, has accumulated an abundance of work for me," Washington observed in February 1784.[2] He was a hands-on manager by nature, but conditions at Mount Vernon accented this trait. "I made no money from my Estate during the nine years away from it," Washington explained, and he needed to right this unsustainable situation.[3] Rich in land and other property, including slaves and uncollectable credits, by war's end Washington was short on hard money and burdened with ongoing expenses for a plantation that seemed only to turn a profit when he managed it closely. He rode the circuit of Mount Vernon's five separate farms every morning, Monday through Saturday, observing his some two hundred workers, most of them black slaves, and trying to keep them on task. Afternoons were spent planning ways to improve his livestock and soil productivity through new methods of scientific farming. And he entertained a steady stream of visitors who arrived, often unannounced, to greet the celebrated general and invariably stayed for midday dinner and the night. "Unless some one pops in unexpectedly," Washington noted in 1798, "Mrs Washington and myself will do what I believe has not been done within the last twenty years by us, that is to set down to dinner by ourselves."[4] This period, of course, covered his years at Mount Vernon following his retirement in 1783.[5] Generous hosts, the Washingtons could not or would not curtail their lavish expenditures. They lived well.

Second, no matter how much he hoped to unload it, Washington still carried the weight of a country on his shoulders. He knew from experience that the Articles of Confederation did not confer enough power on the central government to preserve the union and protect the people. Among his last major acts as commander-in-chief, he sent a circular letter to the states urging them to revise the Articles and offered a plan for a peacetime army. After retiring, he never stopped championing the following themes in public and in private: a strong central government was needed to promote prosperity at home, to maintain respect abroad, and to expand westward. Ongoing developments under the confederation, as the states pulled apart and the economy deteriorated, reconfirmed his fears. As early as 1784 he was complaining to one governor about the "deranged state of public Affairs" and writing to another about expanding national powers: "I have no fears arising from this source; but I have many, & powerful ones indeed which predict the worst consequences from a half starved, limping" confederation.[6] In such letters he showed little sign of settling into a quiet retirement.

Washington's two "retirement" concerns, establishing his own estate and the United States, combined in his vision for the American West. Intent on securing his fortune in land, prior to the war Washington had obtained large undeveloped tracts on the frontier. With peace he sought to capitalize on that investment. And like many other Americans, he viewed the West as key to the country's future, being both an outlet for individual enterprise and the site for national expansion, or as he often termed it, the growth of "a New Empire."[7] In this manner, private and public interest coincided in Washington's postwar commitment to western development with, if his letters are to be believed, the public by then taking precedence.[8] Thus, after spending the first nine months of his so-called retirement trying to restore order to his plantation, Washington headed west to inspect his frontier holdings along the Ohio and Great Kanawha Rivers in what are now West Virginia and southeastern Pennsylvania. This trip, it turned out, crystalized his hopes and fears for the country and drew Washington back into the public sphere. In a sense, his long journey back from retirement to the Constitutional Convention and the presidency began with his trip west in 1784.

THE TRIP BEGAN well enough. Washington set out by horseback on September 1 with three slaves or servants and his longtime friend and physician James Craik for a planned six-week overland trek. Craik's son and Washington's nephew soon joined them. Washington knew roughly what to expect. He had crossed the territory several times as a young surveyor in the 1740s and as a colonial militia officer fighting the French and their Native American allies in the 1750s. On those trips, he had sometimes traveled light and often slept under only a blanket.

Not this time, or at least not at first. Although the party planned to stay in public houses or private homes whenever possible, for nights without lodging they carried an officer's marquee, or grand tent, for the four gentlemen and a horseman's tent for the attendants. Other baggage included bedding, sheets, silver cups and spoons, Madeira and port wine (again for the gentlemen), two kegs of rum for the frontier folk they would encounter, all manner of cooking equipment, assorted spices, extra horseshoes, and Washington's fishing lines.

The party's outbound route followed the Potomac River in a westerly direction from Mount Vernon to Cumberland, Maryland, and then, leaving the river, took a more northerly tack across the Allegheny Mountains on Braddock's Road toward Pittsburgh. The Potomac, which literally cuts through a parallel series of low ridges before turning south at Cumberland, marks the boundary between Virginia and Maryland. On this trip Washington favored the Virginia side, where he owned scattered tracts that he leased to farmers. Trotting on his great horse at a gait of about five miles per hour, Washington reached Cumberland on the trip's tenth day. Opened for settlement by Virginia and Maryland prior to the Revolutionary War, the part of the Potomac valley below Cumberland had become an integral part of the eastern states by 1784. Many of its settlers had cast their lot with the patriot cause in 1776 and now gave Washington a hero's welcome. His tenants, strained by a decade of war and recession, paid what they could toward their long-past-due rents and cheered him on his way. To this point the trip went well.

The troubles began after he left the settled lands east of the Alleghenies and began ascending Braddock's Road into southwestern Pennsylvania. As a colonial militia officer serving under

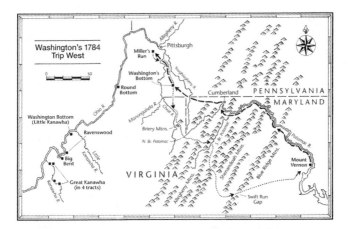

Washington's 1784 trip west, prepared under the author's direction
by Richard H. Britton, mapmaker, for the Fred W. Smith
Presidential Library for the Study of George Washington.
(Used by permission of the Mount Vernon Ladies' Association)

the British general Edward Braddock during the French and
Indian War in 1755, Washington had helped cut this pathway
through the wilderness to support and supply a massive British
assault on French positions in the Ohio valley, and he had re-
treated in haste across it after Braddock's crushing defeat. Now,
twelve days after he left Mount Vernon, the road took him by
Great Meadows, the former site of Fort Necessity, which Washington had surrendered to the French in 1754 and later privately
acquired as investment property.

The autumn rains had begun by this time, turning Braddock's Road into a muddy trough. His tenements at Great
Meadows, Washington noted, were "little improved, tho' capable of being turned to great advantage."[9] In reality, the place
was as much a sodden fen in 1784 as when he had surrendered
it to the French thirty years earlier. Washington had posted the

plots for lease but so far had had no takers. The site was scarcely better for farming than it had been for a fort.

With his baggage bogged down by rain and mud, Washington rushed ahead with a single attendant to reach his much larger tract at a place called Washington's Bottom in time for the scheduled auction of a gristmill that he owned with Gilbert Simpson. Since 1772 Simpson had been Washington's agent in managing this 1,644-acre tract and his partner in developing a farm and mill on part of it. Washington advanced the capital, Simpson provided the labor, and they would share the profits. But there were no profits, or at least none that Simpson reported.

Rarely charitable when it came to business, by 1775 Washington had dismissed Simpson as a man of "extreme stupidity," but being in his first year as commander-in-chief of patriot forces, he had been too preoccupied by war to wind down the partnership.[10] By the Revolutionary War's end in 1783, Washington suspected Simpson of something much worse: fraud. More than anything else, resolving this long-festering dispute with Simpson had prompted Washington's trip west. In July, Washington advertised the farm for lease, its stock and slaves for sale, and the mill for auction. He went west to see these matters through.

Washington was accustomed to having his way with subordinates, and his frustrations only mounted when he encountered his distrusted "partner" on Simpson's home turf. On inspection, the mill, built by Simpson with Washington's money without Washington having seen it, lacked sufficient water power to operate. And the plots leased by Simpson as Washington's agent to individual settlers while Washington was at war offered little promise. The tenants struck Washington as people of a lower order. He collected what he could from them in rent and arranged some new leases, but when he tried to auction the mill, no one bid. It was worthless due to the lack of head. Washington wanted to get out of this place as soon as possible after the auction, but a settled rain forced him to stay on with Simpson for three more nights. If this seemed like purgatory to the business-minded and cash-strapped Washington, then hell awaited at the next stop.

A foretaste of the coming torment arrived while Washington was still with Simpson. It came in the form of Seceders from Washington's 2,813-acre tract at nearby Miller's Run. The American frontier always attracted more than its share of religious groups seeking their Zion in the howling wilderness. Members of one such band, the Seceders, a poor but earnest sect of Scotch-Irish Calvinists, had the misfortune of staking their claim to a frontier haven on land already claimed by the father of their country. Having known for a decade that Washington claimed the land where they squatted, upon learning that he was on his way to assert his rights they sent a delegation to deter and dissuade him. The Seceders "came here to set forth their *pretensions,*" Washington wrote in his diary about this initial meeting, "and to enquire into my rights." But he saw through their pretext of reasonableness and would not concede anything without visiting the tract himself.

When the two sides met again at Miller's Run, both asserted their rights. Such conflicts were common. At the time, claimants to undeveloped land could base their rights either on a government grant, survey, and some improvement or on occupancy, whichever happened first. Washington and most speculators used the former method; the Seceders and many other frontier settlers used the latter. For the Miller's Run tract, Washington had purchased a warrant and then hired a local agent to survey the land in 1771 and to build a small cabin on it in 1772. The tract being otherwise empty, the Seceders had moved onto it in 1773 and claimed the land by occupancy. As if to underscore their intentions, they built one of their buildings so close to the preexisting cabin that its door could not open.

At their Miller's Run confrontation, Washington insisted that the Seceders lease the land from him. They refused but offered to pay a modest price "to avoid contention."[11] Washington favored renting over selling his frontier property because he wanted to oversee its development. As the Seceders recounted their labors in clearing the land and explained their religious convictions against leasing it, Washington softened somewhat. Their hard work and earnest efforts impressed him. Certainly they had improved the land more than his tenants at Washington's Bottom had done. He offered to sell, but the sides could not agree on a fair price. Rather than pay much, the Seceders would fight the validity of Washington's claim in court. Washington devoted considerable time over the next two years to assembling evidence to substantiate his warrant and survey. Both were shaky. In the end, thanks to a good lawyer, Washington won the case and the Seceders moved on with the frontier. (It did not hurt that the judge hearing the case was a signer of the Declaration of Independence and an old friend of Washington.)

From Miller's Run, Washington planned to proceed southwest along the east bank of the Ohio River to a series of smaller and larger holdings he had acquired: Round Bottom (1,293 acres), Washington Bottom or Little Kanawha (2,343), Ravenswood (2,448), Big Bent (4,470), and ultimately Great Kanawha (23,216 acres in four tracts). Washington held the most hope for this last holding, situated as it was on rich bottomland. He viewed it as his best long-term investment. Word had spread of danger ahead, however. "The Indians, it is said, were in too discontented a mood, for me to expose myself to their insults," Washington wrote.[12] They had been provoked by incursions by American settlers onto land northwest of the

Ohio River, "which they claim as their territory," and the failure of Congress to negotiate a peace treaty with them following the Revolutionary War.[13]

Two years earlier, while leading an attack on a native village northwest of the Ohio, Washington's local agent—the one who had "improved" the Miller's Run tract for Washington—had been captured, beaten, scalped alive, and slowly roasted to death. Washington obviously did not want to suffer a similar fate or risk a possible kidnapping for ransom. He considered asking for American soldiers from nearby Fort Pitt to accompany him, but they were too few to engage in such errands or otherwise defend the frontier. "I thought it better to return, than to make a bad matter worse by hazarding abuse from the Savages," he explained.[14] His new local agent later informed Washington that some natives had heard about his intended visit and had set a trap to capture him. As yet another example of Washington's good fortune in battle and other potentially deadly encounters, consider how another course might have changed American history.

HIS TRIP WEST disorientated and disconcerted Washington. It was as if the frontier and its people were conspiring to frustrate his plans for himself and his hopes for his country. The cascading setbacks forced him to confront issues in his personal finances and the nation's future that he might have put off had he stayed at home. On a personal level, his retirement plans relied on income from his large landholdings at Washington's Bottom, Miller's Run, and the Great Kanawha. With America supposedly at peace, Washington had gone west to make these assets profitable in the postwar economy. He found no present potential for revenue from the first, obstinate squatters occupying the second, and hostile native tribes restricting access to the third. Any investor seeking profit on the frontier would have faced similar obstacles. On the public level, Washington came to believe that American prosperity and perhaps even national union required western expansion. Without denying his personal interests in securing the frontier, Washington wrote shortly after his return, "I consider this business in a far more extensive point of view, and the more I have revolved the subject, the more important it appears to me; not only as it respects our commerce, but our political interests, and the well being, and strength of the union."[15]

A lack of national power and resources lay at the heart of the problem, Washington believed. A year had passed since Britain signed the treaty recognizing American sovereignty over the entire region, yet British troops continued to occupy forts northwest of the Ohio River, where they traded with the native peoples for furs and from which they supplied them with guns and ammunition. Set aside by Britain for those natives under the Proclamation of 1763, this district, later known as the Old Northwest Territory, remained under the control of pro-British tribes. With virtually no funds or forces, the US government was powerless to secure the frontier. Moreover, Virginia ceded its claims over the region to Congress in 1784, making its defense a national problem. If Congress could open, sell, and settle these lands and thereby gain authority and revenue, it could bolster the union. If not, it risked losing them to a foreign power, and with them, much of the reason for a national government. This became Washington's fear.

As he saw it, the danger was not limited to territory northwest of the Ohio River but encompassed the entire frontier. "The Western settlers, (I speak now from my own observation) stand as it were upon a pivot," Washington wrote upon his return from the West, "the touch of a feather, would turn them any way."[16] Spain controlled the mouth of the Mississippi and the trans-Mississippi West, he noted, and settlers west of the

Appalachian Mountains from Pennsylvania to Georgia could turn toward it for access to trade. Britain controlled the Great Lakes and the St. Lawrence River, offering another potential trade route for western settlers. Native tribes still occupied virtually the entire territory claimed by the United States west of the Appalachians, and they were protective of their land and more favorably disposed to the British than to the Americans.

Washington detected little loyalty to the United States in the white settlers that he encountered on the frontier. "The ties of consanguinity which are weakening every day will soon be no bond," Washington warned.[17] "If then the trade of that Country should flow through the Mississipi or St Lawrence," he cautioned, "if the Inhabitants thereof should form commercial connexions, which lead, we know, to intercourse of other kinds — they would in a few years be as unconnected with us, indeed more so, than we are with South America."[18] For the good of the country, Washington concluded, the United States must secure the frontier. And he believed that success would require both an American military presence and effective trans-Appalachian commercial communications. "The more [such] communications are opened, the closer we bind that rising world (for indeed it may be so called) to our interest; and the greater strength we shall acquire by it," Washington wrote at the time. "The political object is, in my estimation, immense."[19] He had one particular "communication" principally in mind: Potomac River navigation.

WASHINGTON HAD DREAMED of Potomac River navigation long before independence made it a patriotic cause. Not only could such a waterway improve access to his frontier holdings but it would channel western trade through the mouth of the Potomac near his Mount Vernon plantation. Both would increase his wealth. Following independence, he promoted this

scheme on public as well as private grounds; indeed, those public concerns probably came to predominate in his own motives
for the project. But little had actually changed in Washington's
thinking about it since 1754, when he first suggested using
the Potomac River to carry supplies for General Braddock's
planned assault on French forces in the Ohio valley. When
Braddock had opted for land transport because of the river's
treacherous falls and rapids, a subscription drive had been
launched to raise private funds for improving navigation on
the river below Cumberland. With Washington serving as a
trustee for the enterprise, construction had begun on a bypass
canal around Little Falls, about twenty-five miles upstream
from Mount Vernon, by 1775, before the Revolutionary War
intervened to put the entire project on hold. These rapids stood
at the head of navigation, the first obstacle to upstream travel.
Now Washington wanted to revive that construction effort
and expand upon it.

At the time, no one knew whether navigation could be extended beyond Cumberland, Maryland, along one of the Potomac River's upland tributaries to a practical overland portage
for reaching a navigable branch of the Ohio. The Potomac's
lower part, below Cumberland, would prove problematic
enough, particularly about thirty-five miles above Mount
Vernon at Great Falls, where the river drops seventy-six feet in
less than a mile. But these obstacles were well known and could
be assessed. Not so further upstream.

Accurate maps of the upper Potomac and Ohio River systems simply did not exist, and no one knew the distance between the two networks. Accordingly, on the outbound leg
of his western journey in September 1784, Washington asked
people along the way about the headwaters of the Potomac
and the Ohio and inquired where the two river systems came
closest together. Although their answers often conflicted, he

carefully recorded them in the hope of later determining the best transit route. To reach his frontier holdings, however, Washington's party had left the Potomac River at Cumberland and followed Braddock's overland road into the Ohio valley. His travels cut short before reaching his more remote properties, Washington decided to salvage what he could of the trip by working his way back home through uncharted wilderness in search of waterways.

A gray-haired retired general, America's leading citizen set off on September 22, 1784, from his land at Washington's Bottom for a ten-day cross-country trek across an unknown and unmarked route. He traveled light. Sending back most of his supplies and attendants with James Craik over the conventional route, Washington headed south by southeast on horseback into the wilds with only his nephew, perhaps an attendant or two, and at times a local guide. He followed the Cheat River tributary of the Monongahela at first, looking for its headwaters nearest the Potomac River watershed in the Allegheny Mountains. Stands of mainly white oak covered the rocky hillsides. Washington noted, "In places there are Walnut and Crab tree bottoms, which are very rich."[20] At some points the travelers followed broad trails cut by wandering herds of buffalo, which still populated the region; at others, they simply bushwhacked.

The rain continued off and on throughout the trip, making the way miserable. More than six feet tall, broad in the hips, and riding high on his horse, Washington continually pushed through wet branches that soaked him to the bone. The route went over ridges, through glades, and across streams, roughly thirty-five miles per day in a southerly direction. Even though Washington rarely complained about physical hardships, he did observe at one point in his diary that the Briery Mountains, in present-day West Virginia, were "intolerable" to cross.[21] Traveling without a tent in a region lacking taverns or public houses, the party ate and slept in private homes if possible; outside if not. Imagine the surprise of isolated settlers when the legendary general appeared unannounced at their door in the backwoods. They could never have expected the encounter, nor would they ever forget it. At one remote cabin, Washington noted, "we could get nothing for our horses, and only boiled Corn for ourselves." Still, it was better than the previous night, about which he reported that he had slept in a damp meadow "with no other shelter or cover than my cloak and was unlucky enough to have a heavy shower of Rain."[22]

On September 29, having crossed the Allegheny Mountains and reached the South Branch of the Potomac, which he had planned to follow north to rejoin the rest of his party on the main road, Washington again made a sudden decision to go his own way. If the sole reason for choosing his route home had been to chart waterways for navigation, this was the logical place to turn north, as his way would follow the last likely link between the headwaters of the Ohio and Potomac River systems. Washington must have had some other purpose to extend his backwoods trek. Perhaps it reminded him of his youthful adventures as a frontier surveyor. Perhaps he simply sought solitude. Whatever the reason, sending his nephew north to tell the others, Washington continued southeast over the Shenandoah Mountains to the valley beyond and then turned east across the Blue Ridge at Swift Run Gap to the Piedmont and home. For much of this final portion of his trip, Washington traveled alone or with a single attendant. Parts of the route had no settlers.

The time apart gave him a chance to reflect. "Tho' I was disappointed in one of the objects which induced me to undertake this journey namely to examine into the situation, quality, and advantages of the Land which I hold upon the Ohio and Great Kanawha," Washington wrote in a long entry near the end of his travel diary, "I am well pleased with my journey, as it has been the means of my obtaining a knowledge of the . . . temper and disposition of the Western Inhabitants." Despite their indolence and isolation, he noted, these settlers could be brought into the sphere of American commerce and governance by extending "the inland Navigation as far as it can be done with convenience" in their direction. His explorations proved it possible, Washington assured himself, and suggested a plausible route up the Potomac's North Branch and across a portage to the nearest headwaters of the Ohio, on the Cheat River. It became his cause.[23]

WITHIN WEEKS OF his return to Mount Vernon, Washington sent a shower of letters about the Potomac navigation to influential Virginians and Marylanders. These letters represented such a turning point in Washington's activities that the modern editors of his papers introduce the first of them with the comment that it "marks his return to public life."[24] Certainly they show his political acumen. In this set of letters, Washington boasts of the profits that would flow from western navigation, warns of losing the West without it, and reports on his findings about the feasibility of using a Potomac River route. Unabashedly appealing to the nationalistic concern that largely moved him, he hailed Potomac River navigation as "the cement of interest, to bind all parts of the Union together by indissoluble bonds — especially that part of it, which lies immediately west of us."[25]

With a plan in mind, Washington turned to getting approval from the Virginia and Maryland legislatures for a private toll route on the Potomac and to securing investors for the project. If he had any doubts about his political clout, the next few weeks should have put them to rest. With both the Virginia and Maryland legislatures then in session, Washington shuttled between them to secure approval for a joint-stock company to build and operate the waterway. Despite resistance from self-interested proponents of other routes, he got his way. When it looked as if the two states might pass different bills and thus not create a single company, Washington urged them to appoint commissioners to agree on terms. No sooner asked than done. Virginia tapped Washington and two others. Maryland named a delegation that included three signers of the Declaration of Independence. Washington chaired the meetings, which quickly produced a bill granting everything he wanted. Both state legislatures then passed the bill within days of receiving it. By early January 1785, scarcely four months after his western trip, Washington had his company and soon would be elected its first president. "The earnestness with which he espouses the undertaking is hardly to be described," James Madison noted at the time, "and surely he could not have chosen an occupation more worthy of succeeding to that of establishing the political rights of his Country."[26]

With Washington drumming up interest, private funds flowed into the new company. "Men who can afford to lay a little while out of their money," he wrote to one potential investor, "are laying the foundation of the greatest returns of any speculation I know of in the world."[27] By the middle of 1785 Washington could claim, "Of the £50,000 Sterling required for the Potomac navigation, upwards of £40,000, was subscribed before the middle of May, & increasing fast."[28]

For Washington, the presidency of the Potomac Company became a consuming occupation, though one that he pursued while also managing his plantation and investment properties. He threw himself into deciding between cutting sluices through rapids and digging bypass canals around them, hiring supervisors and workers, and even overseeing the means of operation. On field trips, he frequently canoed down the river's swiftest parts in search of the best place for a channel or to inspect work in progress. "Retirement from the public

Bust of George Washington, by Jean-Antoine Houdon, made
from clay in Mount Vernon, Virginia, 1785, from a life mask.
(Used by permission of Mount Vernon Ladies' Association)

walks of life has not been so productive of the leisure & ease
as might have been expected," Washington wryly remarked to
Benjamin Franklin.[29]

By the autumn of 1785, when Washington sent this remark to
Franklin, the company had separate teams of about fifty workers each cutting navigable channels through two of the Potomac's larger rapids. The task involved digging, pulling, and
blasting rock, sand, and sediment from the riverbed, miserable
work that few freemen would do. At first the company used indentured servants for much of the manual labor, but when they
kept running away, it turned to slaves, whom the company had

better success keeping on task. Progress remained sluggish, though, too slow for Washington. "In a boat we passed down the Seneca [rapids] to the place where the workmen were blowing Rocks," he wrote in one diary entry. "To me it seemed as if we had advanced but little, owing to the fewness, and sickliness of the hands."[30] Still, Washington remained optimistic.

In fact, however, in his work on Potomac River navigation Washington had more success moving human obstacles than he did physical ones. The project was far from finished in 1789, when he resigned as the Potomac Company's president to take the helm of the new American government, yet he never gave up on it and closely followed its progress. Indeed, as the nation's first president he commissioned a painting of Great Falls for the executive residence, and upon retirement he carried it back with him to Mount Vernon, where it hung in the large reception room for his guests to see. Even after it opened for commercial use, the waterway never fulfilled Washington's hopes for it. No one made a fortune on Potomac Company stock; the Erie Canal became the main waterway to and from the West; railroads soon replaced canals in linking the union. Physical impediments such as sheer falls, shallow rapids, and steep slopes doomed Washington's grand vision for Potomac navigation.

Yet if he could not move mountains, the project proved he could move men. Before he stepped down, Washington followed up on his success in getting the company founded and funded with a singular triumph in clearing obstacles to its operation through the adoption in 1785 of the landmark Potomac River compact.

THE PROSPECT OF commercial traffic on the Potomac brought to the fore long-simmering jurisdictional disputes between Virginia and Maryland. Under the Articles of Confederation

Great Falls of the Potomac, by George Beck, 1797.
(Used by permission of Mount Vernon Ladies' Association)

each state was a republic unto itself. It could have its own rules and regulations, taxes and tariffs, and currency. Some states levied imposts on goods from other states. Unless the states cooperated, traveling along an interstate boundary like the Potomac River could impose problems for people and products.

Late in 1784, Virginia and Maryland appointed commissioners to address political barriers to Potomac River commerce. Scheduled to convene in Alexandria, Virginia, on March 21, 1785, for a week of meetings, the conference was threatened by a late-winter snowstorm and confused instructions from Governor Patrick Henry to Virginia's delegates. Ever watchful concerning matters impacting the Potomac Company, Washington invited the commissioners to pursue their deliberations in the warmth of nearby Mount Vernon. A gracious and interested host who liberally lubricated his guests with good wine, Washington made sure that the conference reached agreement on critical matters of tolls, tariffs, and trade. With Washington's support, it went beyond Governor Henry's instructions to also agree on shared contributions for navigational aids, common fishing rights, and cooperation on protecting travelers in the Chesapeake Bay.

Known as the Mount Vernon Compact, its thirteen clauses were ratified by the legislatures of both states, with Madison serving at Washington's behest as floor manager for the bill in Virginia. Inspired by Washington's vision, the two states realized that both benefited from interstate cooperation and that those benefits could multiply if more states participated. "We are either a United people, or we are not," Washington wrote to Madison at the time, and "if the former, let us, in all matters of general concern act as a nation." In this letter, Washington made clear that he saw the United States as "a nation" with "national objects to promote, and a national character to support."[31]

Emboldened by this success, Madison, with Washington's support, took a further step toward uniting the states. At the time, trade disputes like those dividing Maryland and Virginia afflicted many states. Pennsylvania, Delaware, and New Jersey battled over their respective rights to use the Delaware River, for example, while New York, New Jersey, and Connecticut clashed over New York Harbor. Within days after Virginia approved the Mount Vernon Compact, Madison proposed that its legislature call a general meeting on interstate commercial regulations to be attended by delegates from all thirteen states. In response, twelve delegates from five states assembled in Annapolis on September 11, 1786, including Madison and, from New York, Washington's former army aide Alexander Hamilton.

Even before they met, however, Madison, Hamilton, and some other delegates recognized that any convention limited to commercial issues could not resolve the problems facing America. Only a thorough revision of the Articles could achieve that. When the Annapolis meeting failed to attract enough delegates and so could not achieve even its limited goals, Hamilton proposed that those present simply call for a second convention, with a broader mandate, and go home, which is what they did. Some already charged that the Annapolis meeting could have attracted more delegates and achieved more results if Washington had participated, as he had at Mount Vernon. The challenge then became getting him to the proposed second meeting, which was called for the following summer in Philadelphia. Yet those near him could already discern that Washington's great western adventure of 1784 and the Potomac navigation issues it spawned would help to draw him out of retirement and perhaps propel him toward a role in strengthening the federal union.[32] By looking west, Washington more clearly envisioned the future for the United States, a future that realized his dreams of westward expansion.

CHAPTER THREE

Founding Federalism

1786–1787

T HE PENDING Philadelphia convention presented Washington with a dilemma. He had publicly committed to retire permanently from public service following the American Revolution and leave the country's political future to elected leaders. Indeed, this had become a central feature of his public persona as the "American Cincinnatus," honored for his military service and beloved for his devotion to popular rule. Further, the Society of Cincinnati, a fraternal association of Revolutionary War officers originally formed in 1783 at the Newburgh encampment with Washington as its president, by coincidence had scheduled its first triennial meeting for Philadelphia at nearly the same time as the convention. Popular objections to the society's seemingly aristocratic pretensions had led Washington, using his health as pretext, to excuse himself from attending the triennial meeting. Attending the convention would place him in an awkward position with respect to the society, whose members included many friends. Yet his legacy rested on the success of the burgeoning republic stretching from New England to Georgia and west to the Mississippi River that was to arise out of the Revolutionary War and that drew him to Philadelphia.

Founded on the ideal of natural rights for free men, this "United States" represented an utterly novel experiment in large-scale popular rule in a world then dominated by monarchies, theocracies, aristocracies, and dictatorships. Washington suggested as much in his 1783 Circular Letter to the States, issued shortly before the war's end at a time when he despaired over the confederation's inability to pay its troops and repay its creditors. His 1784 trip to inspect his western properties, which showed him the tenuous nature of the new republic's hold on lands west of the Appalachians, reinforced his conviction that the Articles of Confederation, which then looped the states into a loose alliance, must be revised to give the central government effective control over interstate commerce, foreign affairs, national defense, and its own revenue. To Washington, these were essential to promote liberty, protect property, and preserve independence.

The individual states did not and could not offer a suitable alternative, Washington believed. First, as he often noted, the Revolutionary War had been won by no single state, but by the United States as a whole, and if those states did not remain united, that independence could be lost — not because Britain did not recognize each state as independent but because foreign powers could pick them off one by one as circumstances allowed. Second, if left to act in their own interests, the states would squabble among themselves to the detriment of the American people. In particular, Washington believed that one central authority should govern interstate and international commerce. Third and perhaps most important, many states were failing to protect individual liberty and private property. The breakdown of public order in some states, the reckless emission of paper money by others, and the worsening economic conditions everywhere during the postwar period deepened Washington's concerns and those of like-minded Americans. They shared those concerns among themselves in countless private letters. In Washington's case, they were evident in his correspondence with New York's John Jay, the confederation's brilliant but beleaguered foreign secretary.

Early in 1786 Jay sent a desperate appeal to Washington begging him to emerge from retirement long enough to lead the effort for constitutional reform. "Experience has pointed out Errors in our national Government, which call for Correction, and which threaten to blast the Fruit we expected from our 'Tree of Liberty,'" Jay warned. "An opinion begins to prevail that a general convention for revising the articles of Confederation would be expedient. Whether the People are yet ripe for such a Measure, or whether the System proposed to be attained by it, is only to be expected from Calamity & Commotion, is difficult to ascertain."[1] The caution here referred to Jay's worry that despite all the evident problems with lodging sovereignty in the separate states, popular opposition to centralized power, rooted in colonial experiences of oppression by the British Parliament and Crown, might cause the people to cling to the current defective arrangement until utter chaos resulted and perhaps even political freedom was lost.

Jay then made his plea. To save "the Sovereignty and Independence which Providence has enabled You to be so greatly & gloriously instrumental in securing," he implored, referring to Washington's legacy in securing liberty for the United States, if a convention were called, "I am fervent in my Wishes, that it may comport with the Line of Life you have marked out for yourself, to favor your country with your counsels on such an important & single occasion."[2] In Jay's usage here, of course, *country* meant the United States, not any individual state.

Washington took Jay's concerns seriously—indeed, there was no one he trusted more on such matters—but he also shared Jay's caution about timing. Thus he put him off. "I coincide perfectly in sentiments with you, my dear sir, that there are errors in our National Government which call for correction," Washington wrote, "but my fear is that the people are not yet sufficiently misled to retract from error!" He blamed the situation on ignorance among the people regarding the dangers to freedom and property from the excesses of democracy in some states, especially in those that had lodged too much power in popularly elected officials without sufficient protections for minority rights, and from the wickedness of demagogues who sought to profit from those excesses. "Ignorance & design are difficult to combat," Washington wrote. "Out of these proceed illiberality, *improper* jealousies, and a train of evils which oftentimes, in republican governments, must be sorely felt before they can be removed."[3]

Agreeing with Jay that "something must be done, or the fabric must fall," Washington remained uncertain whether the time had come to act. "I scarcely know what opinion to entertain of a general Convention," he cautioned. "That it is necessary to revise, and amend the articles of Confederation, I entertain *no* doubt; but what may be the consequences of such an attempt *is* doubtful." Washington feared that if he participated in a failed convention, he might use up precious amounts of political capital and lessen his ability to intervene effectively later. He preferred to wait until the calamitous consequences of the current course became clear to all people of goodwill. "Virtue, I fear, has, in a great degree, taken its departure from our Land," he wrote in most dispirited terms, "and the want of disposition to do justice is the source of the national embarrassments."[4]

THE ANXIETY OVER constitutional reform reflected in this exchange between a New York patrician and a Virginia planter betrayed far more fundamental concerns than mere fears of losing the West, simple hopes for a national market economy, and plain desires to repay government creditors, though those issues certainly weighed heavily on both men. Their letters spoke in terms of calamity and commotion, loss of public virtue and disposition to do justice, and breakdown of the so-cial fabric under the excesses of majority faction. Liberty itself was at risk, both men declared, much as it had been in 1776. But this time the threat came from within, which made it worse.

The news reaching Mount Vernon from other states trou-bled Washington greatly. A debtors' insurrection led in part by former Revolutionary War officers, including most famously Daniel Shays, closed the courts in Massachusetts until its forc-ible suppression by a creditor-funded militia commanded by Washington's second-in-command at the Siege of Yorktown, Benjamin Lincoln. The wholesale printing of devalued paper money by debtor-dominated Rhode Island undercut property rights in a manner that threatened to spread widely to other states. Open rebellion against New York rule in Vermont raised the prospect of disintegrating the union, especially after the rebels there sought support from British Canada and welcomed Shays and other insurgents from Massachusetts. Native Amer-icans had effectively closed the Ohio country to American settlement, and they were pushing back the frontier in Geor-gia, with the toothless confederation government powerless to stop them. Whatever a balanced historical perspective might conclude about these events today, as presented to Washington in the procreditor newspapers that he read and by excited cor-respondents whom he knew and trusted, such as Jay, Lincoln, and Henry Knox, they looked catastrophic.

The events caused Washington to wonder whether Amer-icans were capable of self-government. "Who besides a tory could have foreseen, or a Briton predict them!" he wrote in late 1786 to Knox, the confederation's secretary of war and Washing-ton's wartime chief subordinate. "Notwithstanding the boasted virtue of America, we are far gone in every thing ignoble & bad."[5] And so Washington wrote in November 1786 to the Vir-ginia congressman James Madison, who was already thinking about a new national political structure, "Thirteen Sovereignties pulling against each other, and all tugging at the federal head, will soon bring ruin to the whole; whereas a liberal, and energetic Constitution, well guarded & closely watched, to prevent incroachments, might restore us to that degree of respectability & consequence, to which we had a fair claim."[6] Fiercely proud of his country and its experiment in self-government, Washington was mortified.

In March 1787, three months after the disturbances in Massachusetts died down, Washington wrote to his former aide and foreign confidant the Marquis de Lafayette about their ongoing impact on the campaign for constitutional reform. "These disorders are evident marks of a defective government," Washington asserted. "Indeed, the thinking part of the people of this Country are now so well satisfied of this fact that most of the Legislatures have appointed, & the rest it is said will appoint, delegates to meet at Philadelphia the second Monday in May next in general Convention of the States to revise, and correct the defects of the federal System."[7]

By this time, Virginia had picked Washington to lead its delegation to that convention, and he was debating with himself and others whether he should go. His main worries were that the convention had been called merely to propose amendments to the Articles of Confederation, not to frame a fundamentally new constitution, and that the people might not yet be ready to accept the needed overhaul. He did not want to waste his time and political capital tinkering with a failed system. "A thorough reform of the present system is indispensable, and with hand and heart I hope the business will be essayed in the full Convention," Washington now wrote to Madison, who had also been tapped by Virginia to attend. Fearing that some states might impose limits on their delegates, Washington reiterated his hope that the convention "would probe the defects of the Constitution to the bottom, and provide radical cures."[8] Washington was no radical, yet only on these terms would he go to Philadelphia for the key act in what some historians would later call America's peaceful "second revolution" of 1787–88.[9]

Agonizing over how to proceed, Washington wrote to Jay, Knox, and Madison requesting their advice on a restructured government. This was how Washington liked to lead. As a general, for example, he had typically convened a council of his officers before battle and listened more than he spoke. Only after hearing their advice, and appreciating that some of them knew more about certain matters than he did, would Washington choose his course. In this instance, struck by the similarities of the responses he had received, in April 1787 Washington prepared an abstract comparing them.[10] All three of these confederation leaders envisioned a truly national government for the United States with separate legislative, judicial, and executive branches. All would divide Congress into an elite upper house and a popular lower house. Madison elaborated more than the others on the judiciary. He viewed a system of supreme and inferior courts reaching into every state as essential to avoid local bias in expounding national laws and deciding cases involving citizens of different states. Madison wrote less than the others about the executive, though he had invested more time than the others in studying the concept of balanced government.[11] Indeed, at this point Madison worried more about a propensity toward monarchy in ruling over expansive territory than he did about the need for a strong executive, and he had to be brought around to the view that the presidency could serve as an effective check on Congress.[12]

Like Jay and Knox, Madison was obsessed with reining in the states. "The national government should be armed with positive and compleat authority in all cases which require uniformity," he told Washington, "such as the regulation of trade." He recommended placing state militias under national control and suggested that, as in colonial days, the central government should appoint state governors. Recognizing the inexpediency of abolishing the states altogether, however, Madison called for a federal system — "some middle ground," he called it — "which may at once support a due supremacy of the national authority on issues of general concern, yet not exclude the state authorities whenever they can be subordinately useful." He maintained that in areas under its domain the national government must have the power to act directly on the people, not just through the states, and that the "individual independence" of the states could not be reconciled with the "idea of aggregate sovereignty."[13] All three agreed on this key point.

In his responses to Knox, Jay, and Madison, Washington embraced their proposals and made them his own. "Those enumerated in your letter are so obvious, & sensibly felt that no logick can controvert," Washington told Jay. "But, is the public mind matured for such an important change?" Expressing similar sentiments to Knox, Washington stated his fear that "the political machine will yet be much tumbled & tossed, and possibly wrecked altogether, before such a system as you have defined, will be adopted." Washington apparently said much the same to Madison when the two met at Mount Vernon. Jealous of power, state officials "would give their weight of opposition to such a revolution," Washington predicted. Nevertheless, he wrote to Jay, he wished to try this convention route and find out "what can be effected." It might represent "the last peaceable mode" of saving the republic.[14] And should it devise a vigorous new constitution under his leadership, Knox assured Washington, he would have doubly earned "the glorious republican epithet — The Father of Your Country."[15] These aging revolutionaries were again conspiring in revolutionary terms.

Make no mistake about it, Washington was reluctant to go, but as when he had volunteered to lead the patriot army against Britain, he was inexorably drawn to the field of action where and when he thought he could make a difference. Once the chance to leave a legacy became clear in this case, he went. Americans understood this and discussed its significance. "It is with particular satisfaction we inform the public, that our illustrious fellow Citizen, GEORGE WASHINGTON, Esquire, has consented to serve on the ensuing Federal Convention," the *Connecticut Journal* reported on May 2. "What happy consequence may not all the true friends to federal government promise themselves?"[16] Calling him "the American Fabius," after the legendary Roman general and statesman, a Rhode Island paper printed a poem on May 5 about Washington's much anticipated arrival in Philadelphia:

The hero comes, each voice resound his praise,
No envious shafts can dare to chill his rays;
All hail! great man! who, for thy country's cause,
Flew at her call for to protect the laws.[17]

These and other widely circulated accounts show that even before it began, with Washington in charge, Americans expected radical cures from the convention. "Upon the events of this great council, indeed, depends every thing that can be essential to the dignity and stability of the national character," the *Maryland Chronicle* noted in an article dated the very day that Washington passed through Baltimore on his way to the convention.[18] He was greeted in Philadelphia with an essay in one leading local paper that proposed giving Congress complete power over "those things which alike concern all the states."[19] "The more we abridge the states of their sovereignty, and the more supreme power we concentrate in an Assembly of the States," an essayist in a Philadelphia newspaper observed in late May, "the more safety, liberty, and prosperity will be enjoyed by each of the states."[20]

REFLECTING HIS commitment to serve, Washington was one of the few delegates to arrive on time in Philadelphia. He duly went to the State House at the appointed hour on May 14 to find only Madison and the Pennsylvanians present. They returned daily as other delegates trickled in, but it took ten more days to obtain a quorum.

In the meantime, meeting privately, the Virginians present and apparently the Pennsylvanians cobbled together the outline for a new plan of government. It became known as the Virginia Plan because the Virginia governor, Edmund Randolph, offered it at the convention. Little is known about these meetings, but letters from those present suggest that Washington attended each one and supported the outcome. To the extent that it was his plan, it was the product of a committee, though history has given Madison much of the credit for being its architect. As one Virginian depicted the still forming plan, nothing less than a revolution in government was brewing. "The most prevalent Idea," he wrote, "seems to be a total Alternation of the present federal System and substituting a great National Council . . . with full legislative Powers upon all the Objects of the Union."[21] This sentence effectively summarized the Virginia Plan. People would replace states as the building blocks of a national republic, and Congress would no longer go hat in hand to the states for everything. On matters of national interest—the key qualification here being *national*—the new government would either dictate to the states or deal directly with the people.

When the convention did obtain a quorum, it promptly chose Washington as its president and turned to the matter of rules. Those rules provided that so long as it was represented, each state would have one vote; a majority of states represented could carry a vote; and most controversially, secrecy would obtain throughout. With windows shuttered and doors closed, the members met day after day, six days a week, for more than three months. Individuals came and went, and states gained and lost representation. Delegates from New Hampshire, for example, did not appear until late July, by which time the New Yorkers had left. Rhode Island never sent delegates. As a result, no more than eleven states were represented at any one time, and never more than six votes were needed to pass anything as long as the result was not so objectionable to some as to threaten a breakdown of the whole. Of the seventy-three delegates appointed to the convention, fifty-five attended at some point, thirty-nine signed the document (one in absentia), and only two, Washington and Madison, attended every session. With secrecy strictly enforced, the sole records of the proceedings were in Madison's extensive legislative diary, or "notes," which he kept private for a generation and revised over time; a scattering of diary entries, notes, and letters written by various other delegates; and the official journal of motions and votes.

The silence engulfing the Constitutional Convention especially limits what is known about Washington's role, because as the presiding officer, he rarely spoke on substantive matters inside the hall, where Madison selectively recorded the debate. Washington did talk privately with other members, and he voted with the Virginia delegation.[22] He also supervised the deliberations and called on members when they spoke. But no one recorded these utterances, and obeying the secrecy rule, Washington did not repeat them in letters or other writings. Given his character, he almost certainly listened more than he spoke, which typically gave his words more weight when he did comment.

From his private comments and telltale gestures, other members likely divined where Washington stood on important matters. However, beyond his longstanding and oft-stated desire to create a central government with power to tax, maintain armed

forces, and regulate interstate and international commerce—
positions that he had publicly championed since 1783—the
record of Washington's specific contributions to the Constitution remains frustratingly oblique. Later generations can only
surmise them from the clues available.[23] But those clues are
revealing, especially his often decisive vote within the Virginia
delegation. In the end, for example, it was his tie-breaking vote
that allowed Virginia to endorse the Constitution. Yet his leadership was apparent from the outset.

One day after the convention committed itself to secrecy,
the Virginia delegation dropped its bombshell. Having participated in preparing it, Washington clearly conspired in the
timing of its delivery. To begin "the main business" of the
convention, as Madison termed it in his notes, Washington
called on Randolph.[24] The Virginia governor then presented
his delegation's plan for a new constitution. Once he took the
floor, Randolph held it for most of the day, and he left no doubt
about his state's radical intentions.

As presented by Randolph, the plan contained the outline
for a "national" government made up of a two-house legislature, some sort of chief executive, and a judiciary with supreme
and inferior courts. This represented his delegation's radical
cure for America's woefully inadequate central government.
Citing the discord among the states, the rebellion in Massachusetts, "the havoc of paper money," and its failure to pay
its debts, Randolph argued that the old confederation did
not work and raised "the prospect of anarchy from the laxity
of government every where." Further, he added, "there were
many advantages, which the U.S. might acquire, which were
not attainable under the confederation—such as a productive
impost—counteraction of the commercial regulations of other
nations—pushing of commerce." The hope, Randolph said, lay
in a national government with power to legislate on matters of

general concern and compel obedience. One skeptical delegate captured the speech's essence in a scribble: "Sovereignty is the integral Thing—We ought to be one Nation."[25]

VIRGINIA HAD STAKED its ground, forcing others to respond. No delegate could doubt where Washington stood. He remained a voting member of Virginia's delegation, called on Randolph to speak first, and never suffered any interruption of what one critic called the governor's "long and elaborate speech."[26] Clearly Washington sided with Virginia and its plan. In doing so, he helped to hijack the convention. Congress had endorsed this gathering as a meeting to draft amendments to the Articles of Confederation; Washington's Virginia instead proposed using it to scrap the existing government and forge a nation. That night he likely worked on the long letter that he posted the next day to the American ambassador in Paris, Thomas Jefferson. "The business of this Convention is as yet too much in embryo to form any opinion of the result," Washington wrote. "That something is necessary, all will agree; for the situation of the General Government (if it can be called a government) is shaken to its foundations—and liable to be overset by every blast. In a word, it is at an end, and unless a remedy is soon applied, anarchy & confusion will inevitably ensue."[27] These worried words echoed Randolph's urgent speech.

After heatedly debating and narrowly defeating a motion to limit the proceedings to amending the Articles of Confederation, the convention accepted the Virginia Plan as the starting point for its deliberations and never looked back. Washington sat silent in the hall but surely spoke in private. "Persuaded I am that the primary cause of all our disorders lies in the different State Governments," he soon noted in a letter sent to a fellow Virginian, "and in the tenacity of that power which pervades

the whole of their systems." So long as the states retained "independent sovereignty," he wrote, the country would falter.[28]

The initial battle won, the war then raged over the precise
structure and powers of Congress, the nature of the executive,
the establishment of inferior federal courts, protections for
state-sanctioned slavery, and myriad other matters. Washington again remained silent but wrote privately, "The Men who
oppose a strong & energetic [central] government are, in my
opinion, narrow minded politicians, or are under the influence
of local views."[29] Of all the delegates, it was Alexander Hamilton, of New York, and Pennsylvania's James Wilson — two
probusiness nationalists with close ties to Washington — who
most vocally defended an open-ended grant of power to the
central government. On June 18, for example, after New Jersey
proposed a limiting list of powers in its alternate plan for a federal government, Hamilton exploded. "The general power . . .
must swallow up the State powers, otherwise it will be swal-
lowed up by them," he declared. "Between the National &
State Legislatures," he added, "the former must therefore have
indefinite authority." Wilson was more discreet. Distancing
himself from Hamilton's extreme remarks, he still argued that
the states should only survive as "lesser jurisdictions" or "sub-
divisions" of the nation.[30]

From start to finish, Washington presided at the convention
without formally expressing his views on the proper extent of
the central government's power. He did not need to. Ever since
his 1783 Circular to the States, which was then the country's best-
known public document after the Declaration of Independence,
Washington stood as the personification of nationalism in the
United States. His daily presence on the dais gave weight to the
Virginia Plan, which implicitly bore his imprimatur. If it was
the work of a committee, or even mostly drafted by Madison,
it was no less Washington's work than any Revolutionary War

battle he had won through tactics devised by his officers and executed by his soldiers. And when Randolph drafted a broad enumeration of congressional powers that the Virginia delegation backed as a qualification of the unlimited grant set forth in the Virginia Plan, it included every one that Washington had publically endorsed — especially after Washington's ally James Wilson appended the necessary and proper clause to it.

No issue mattered more to Washington than the central government's sovereignty over matters of common concern. There were other topics for the members to address, some so divisive as to nearly derail the convention, others that every delegate knew would directly impact Washington should he lead the resulting government. They would look to him on these issues too, and he in turn helped to shape the outcome, but national supremacy mattered most to him. "Vain is it to look for respect from abroad, or tranquility at home," Washington wrote one day before the delegates approved Randolph's list of enumerated powers, "till the wisdom and force of the Union can be more concentred."[31]

The nationalists at the convention hall did not win every battle, and the losses of some battles discouraged the most ardent of them. The Senate's composition was the signal loss, a compromise that enraged Hamilton and Madison but not realists like Washington and Benjamin Franklin. The Virginia Plan had called for proportional representation in the House of Representatives and for that body to select the Senate, which would have allowed members from four or five big states to dominate the whole. The Articles of Confederation had given one vote in Congress to each state, with the members casting that vote subject to direction, recallable at will, and paid by their state. Several of the small states benefiting from this allocation of power had instructed their convention delegates to maintain it in the Constitution.

From the outset, everyone must have realized that the logical compromise had the House of Representatives allocated by population and the Senate by state, but it took two months and dueling threats to walk out before both sides agreed. Although Connecticut's Roger Sherman got much of the credit for this so-called Great Compromise, it was apparently big-state pragmatists like Franklin, Washington, and the Pennsylvania delegate Gouverneur Morris who brokered the deal. Indeed, throughout the proceedings, Morris most often served as Washington's surrogate when compromise was called for, since the General's other closest confidants — Madison, Hamilton, and Wilson — tended to hold faster to their principles than Morris. But Morris got the last laugh by working into the Constitution that senators, although appointed by the states, would serve long, fixed terms and be paid by the United States, foreseeing that these factors would likely make them identify more with the nation than with their states. Still, it was enough of a compromise for supporters of the final draft to call themselves federalists rather than nationalists — another politically savvy move. Under this banner, they seized the rhetorical middle ground.

Then it came down to slavery, the issue that most threatened to derail the convention and split the union asunder. Already many northern delegates like Morris and Hamilton hated the institution, while many southern delegates were wedded to it. Washington sided with Virginia and slavery, of course, while Franklin had founded the nation's first abolition society. Yet each was ultimately a pragmatist, and together with other delegates they backed compromises — most notably the Three-Fifths Compromise, protections for the slave trade, and provisions for returning fugitive slaves — that kept every state in the hall and pacified the southerners. If those compromises leaned more toward slavery than necessary, as some historians have argued, perhaps Washington tipped the balance.[32] Certainly the

Three-Fifths Compromise helped to keep Congress and the presidency in southern hands longer than the natural growth of population would have justified. Even more than the Great Compromise, protections afforded slavery revealed the type of federalism that the framers favored. While matters like interstate commerce and foreign affairs and all things necessary and proper to their execution fell within the nation's domain, social arrangements, even the most nefarious, remained with the states. Of course, one person's social arrangements are another's interstate commerce, but such matters were left to be worked out over time and by amendments.

AS THE GREAT COMPROMISE and the Three-Fifths Compromise suggest, there is abundant evidence of Washington's influence in shaping various provisions of the Constitution and securing the compromises that kept the convention on track, but his role in crafting the executive offers as good an example as any of the part he played in Philadelphia. Since everyone presumed that Washington would become the new government's first executive, no one could conceive of the position without thinking about him in it. Indeed, within the year, South Carolina's Pierce Butler flatly stated that his colleagues at the convention "shaped their Ideas and Powers to be given to the President, by their opinions of [Washington's] Virtue."[33]

The presidency was the convention's most original creation. Groping for analogies while debating it, delegates at various times alluded to the Venetian Republic's doge, the Holy Roman Emperor, the king of Poland, the consuls of ancient Rome, and even the pope as examples of political leaders chosen by some sort of elite electorate. None of these analogies fit. The American presidency was something new under the sun.

Having agreed to begin their deliberations by working through the Virginia Plan, the delegates reached the plan's two resolutions regarding the executive on June 1. Perhaps because

Washington was sitting among them, when the delegates reached these resolutions, they fell silent. With the provisions coming from Washington's delegation, no one seemed inclined to dispute them. Washington would be the first president, of course, and the delegates seemed reluctant to cross him.[34] But who would follow Washington? Pennsylvania's chief executive, Benjamin Franklin, broke the silence. Observing that the structure of the executive was "of great importance," he urged the delegates to "deliver their sentiments on it before the question was put."[35] These comment burst the dam, and debate flooded the room. Four days later, with the discussion still going strong, Franklin could add with reference to Washington and the debate over the executive, "The first man, put at the helm would be a good one. No body knows what sort may come afterwards."[36]

The members debated the executive at length three separate times during the convention. In June, during the first of these occasions, they raised virtually all of the issues about the presidency that would later occupy them, but they had trouble even resolving whether one person or a committee should hold the office. With Washington in the room, a unitary executive should have seemed obvious to all, especially since every state had but one governor. Fearful of investing too much power in any single person, however, some delegates—including two from Virginia—favored an executive triumvirate like those of late republican Rome. Denouncing a single executive as "the fetus of monarchy," Randolph averred that "the people" would oppose it.[37] Further, Washington's neighbor and fellow Virginia delegate George Mason added, an executive troika could better represent the country's three regions than any one ruler.[38]

These comments on a unitary executive, coming as they did from old friends, surely vexed Washington, who prided himself on his republican virtue, public support, and unbiased nationalism. Every delegate who knew him well must have understood that Washington would never consent to serving as one member of an executive triumvirate, nor would he be suited for such a post. While he remained silent, others rallied to defend the sort of unitary executive that Washington was so clearly qualified to fill. "Unity in the Executive" would promote "vigor and dispatch" in office, Wilson noted, and by fixing responsibility on one person, would serve as "the best safeguard against tyranny."[39] Elbridge Gerry, of Massachusetts, who had served with Washington in the Continental Congress, stressed that a troika would be especially troublesome in war. "It would be a general with three heads," he declared.[40]

These positions came out in the course of the formal debate, but delegates discussed them on other occasions as well. Like Washington, some members regularly attended evening teas and balls, where they could talk in semiprivate settings. Even those delegates who did not circulate in high society inevitably spent considerable time together outside the Assembly Room. Most of them lived tightly packed into a handful of the city's best boardinghouses and inns, where they dined at common tables.

While he stayed in a private home where he could dine in, Washington frequently ate out with other members. Indeed, on June 2, after the extent of disagreement over the power and structure of the executive first became apparent, Washington ate with the delegates at City Tavern, where the subject of the day's heated debate likely came up and surely remained on everyone's mind. While in session earlier that day, the members raised and could not resolve whether the United States should have one executive officer or three. But later that day, as many of those delegates casually dined with the man who would be that king, Washington's presence must have reassured them. As a frequent guest at City Tavern, the South Carolina delegate

Pierce Butler may have been present. If so, it might explain his later comment that powers vested in the executive would not "have been so great had not many of the members cast their eyes toward General Washington as President."[41] At the convention's next session, the states voted by a margin of seven to three for a single executive. Virginia joined the majority, with Washington casting the deciding vote.[42]

Crafting the presidency in Washington's image did not end with the vote to have a unitary executive but extended over the course of the summer as delegates piled powers on that office far beyond what anyone could have expected given Americans' experience with abuses by the king and royal governors. Of course the president was charged with executing the laws — all state governors had this duty — but in line with Washington's past service, the president was also made commander-in-chief of the nation's armed forces and of the state militias when called into national service. This power had not been in the Virginia Plan, nor had a presidential veto, which was added next. In a provision that both reflected Washington's style of military leadership and underscored the unitary nature of executive power, the Constitution also expressly authorized the president to "require the Opinion, in writing, of the principal Officers in each of the executive Departments, upon any Subject relating to the Duties of their respective Offices."[43]

Further aggrandizement of the presidency came in August. In a major shift, the delegates charged the president with making treaties and appointing judges and ambassadors, subject only to the Senate's advice and consent — powers that they at first had entrusted to the Senate alone. Also in August, they opted to have the president chosen by electors selected for that purpose and eligible for reelection, rather than chosen by Congress for a single term as provided in the Virginia Plan and initially approved by the convention. More than any other change, the status afforded the American executive by independent election for multiple fixed terms, which would differ from the norm for parliamentary republics elsewhere, created an office of enormous potential power—virtually an elected monarch, as some critics complained then and thereafter. Yet it also became one that could effectively check and balance Congress. On every known occasion, Washington voted to strengthen the presidency.

SO IT WENT week after week as Washington successfully guided the convention to its historic conclusion in September, when all the remaining states voted for the Constitution even though some delegates, objecting to parts of it, refused to sign it. The delegates then approved a cover letter and two accompanying resolutions for publicly transmitting the finished draft to Congress. "The friends of our country have long seen and desired, that the power of making war, peace, and treaties, that of levying money and regulating commerce, and the corresponding executive and judiciary authorities should be *fully* and effectually vested in the general government," the letter stated. These factors, it claimed, justified "the *consolidation* of our Union, in which is involved our prosperity, felicity, safety, perhaps our *national* existence."[44] This letter effectively opened the public campaign for ratification. The accompanying resolutions asked Congress to forward the Constitution to the states and, if they ratified it, to set a time for choosing presidential electors and a date for the new government to assume power. Washington's signature on the cover letter and accompanying resolutions assured that they would command attention. Indeed, to the public it looked as if the Constitution came from him, which was its backers' intent. All that remained was for the delegates to ceremonially sign the document.

As the two larger-than-life leaders whose support made the convention and the Constitution credible, Washington and Franklin took center stage for the signing on September 17,

Detail from *Scene at the Signing of the Constitution of the United States,* by Howard Chandler Christy, 1940. (Used by permission of Architect of the Capitol)

1787. They do so in the monumental painting of the event by Howard Chandler Christy that a later Congress commissioned for the United States Capitol. The shutters symbolically open and drapes pulled to reveal a bright new day that backlights the figures in an almost holy aura, Franklin sits facing the viewer at the center surrounded by the other signers. Washington stands alone in near profile to the viewer's right, towering over all others as he surveys the scene from an overly elevated dais.

Christy invented the arrangement of characters and tinkered with the cast, but the painting's spirit rings true. Washington oversaw the signing much as he had the convention, by supervising events from his elevated chair. He called on Franklin first. "I agree to this Constitution with all its faults, if they be such; because I think a general Government necessary for us, and there is no form of Government but what may be a blessing to the people if well administered, and believe farther that this is likely to be well administered for a course of years," Franklin explained with a verbal nod toward Washington as the presumed first president. The alternative, he said, was disunion, with the states "only to meet hereafter for the purpose of cutting one another's throats."[45] Despite the secrecy rule, this speech promptly made it into the newspapers along with Washington's transmittal letter. The great men had spoken for all Americans to hear. At the time, they were widely credited as the Constitution's principal drafters.

Although observed by no one except the convention's members and officers, the signing may have seemed as historic to them as it looks in Christy's painting. Washington signed first and above the rest in a bold, large hand somewhat reminiscent of John Hancock's already well known signature on the Declaration of Independence: "G°: Washington, Presid^t and Deputy from Virginia." Then the other thirty-eight signers filed forward by state, beginning with New Hampshire's John Langdon and proceeding southward to Abraham Baldwin of Georgia. While the last members were signing, Franklin looked at the half sun adorning the crown of Washington's chair. "I have," he said to those near him, "often in the course of the Session, and the vicissitudes of my hopes and fears as to its issue, looked at that behind the President without being able to tell whether it was rising or setting: But now at length I have the happiness to know that it is a rising and not a setting Sun."[46] Madison chose this anecdote involving the Sage of Philadelphia and Washington's chair to close his notes on the convention.

Elaborating somewhat, Washington reported in his diary, "The Members adjourned to the City Tavern, dined together and took a cordial leave." Three days earlier, Washington had enjoyed a farewell reception at the same site hosted by the local city cavalry. The bill has survived and lists as many bottles of Madeira and claret as there were people present, plus large quantities of beer and a substantial charge for breakage. The bill for September 17 does not survive, but if similar, then the leave was indeed cordial. In his diary for the seventeenth, Washington added that after dinner he "retired to meditate on the momentous work which had been executed."[47] The product of that labor—the Constitution—*if* ratified, would transform the rest of his life and his country forever. One step done, a step that Washington soon characterized as "little short of a miracle,"[48] more steps lay ahead, with the General deeply invested in each.

CHAPTER FOUR

Launching a Nation

1787–1789

IN PERHAPS THE most famous scene of American history, George Washington presided over the signing of the United States Constitution on September 17, 1787. A second celebrated scene took place on April 30, 1789, when he took the oath of office as the first president. These two dates bracket a time of rising national partisanship, when Washington displayed the same reserved style of effective leadership in launching the nation that he had shown as commander-in-chief during the American Revolution and that would later mark his presidency. Here, as much as in any other period, later generations can take the measure of the man.

One day after delegates signed the Constitution and sent it to Congress for submission for ratification by conventions of elected representatives in each state, Washington left Philadelphia for his beloved Mount Vernon, ostensibly to let the people work their will. Indeed, on that very day he wrote about the Constitution that "the General opinion on, or reception of it is not for me to decide," and he vowed not to "say anything for or against" it in public.[1] That vow clearly did not extend to private lobbying, however. Scarcely two days after reaching Mount Vernon, Washington sent copies of the document to three former Virginia governors along with identical letters urging them to support it. "I sincerely believe it is the best that could be obtained at this time," he wrote. "If nothing had been agreed to anarchy would soon have ensued."[2] These were just the first in a steady stream of such appeals sent to leaders throughout the United States but particularly in Virginia.

Two of the state's delegates to the Constitutional Convention having refused to sign the document and others lining up behind them, Washington feared that the Constitution would face strong headwinds in Virginia.[3] As much as he wanted to remain above politics and not appear to peddle a document that could lead to his elevation as president, Washington had so much time and reputation invested in the Constitution, and believed so strongly that his country could not survive without it, that its progress consumed him even as he resumed day-to-day management of his estate. Like most federalists, he was convinced that the choice lay between the Constitution and chaos; the preservation of liberty and property required ratification, and ratification necessarily would involve him.

ONCE THE CONVENTION adjourned, news of the Constitution and calls for its ratification spread across the land. Both inevitably focused on Washington's role as president of the convention. "Is it possible that the deliverer of our country would have recommended an unsafe form of government?" a widely reprinted newspaper article asked.[4] Everywhere, early reports sounded much the same. Federalists would rely on the public's trust in Washington to carry the day.[5]

Washington knew the role that his name and reputation were playing in the campaign for ratification. He followed the unfolding drama through private letters and in the newspapers from around the country that he received and read daily. These reports carried endless references to Washington's central role at the Constitutional Convention. "I am convinced that if you had not attended the Convention," the Pennsylvania delegate Gouverneur Morris wrote to Washington in October, "and the same paper had been handed out to the World, it would have met with a colder Reception, fewer and weaker Advocates, and with more and more strenuous opponents."[6] "The universal popularity of General Washington," the New York delegate Alexander Hamilton added, was the key factor in the federalists' favor going into the ratification contests.[7]

Most people likely cared less that Washington had signed the Constitution than that he would presumably lead the government under it. No sooner had the convention issued its Constitution in September than the *Pennsylvania Gazette* proclaimed, "GEORGE WASHINGTON has already been destined, by a thousand voices, to fill the place of the first President."[8] If anything, the *Gazette*'s count was far too low. People everywhere, when they heard about the proposed new government, simply assumed that Washington would lead it.[9] "What will tend more than any thing to the adoption of the new system," the General's former military aide David Humphreys wrote to Washington in September from Connecticut, "will be an universal opinion of your being elected President."[10] No doubt Washington saw it coming, and without coveting or courting the position, he never denied that he would accept it. "Should the Idea prevail that you would not accept the Presidency," Morris warned about the Constitution's prospect, "it would prove fatal in many Parts."[11] By keeping silent, Washington played his part. Even with him in their camp, federalists faced the daunting task of securing ratification for their radical shift of power from the states to the nation.

Federalists had the advantage of a document designed to address the grave economic and political problems then facing the country and influential supporters returning from the convention to each state pushing for ratification. But led at first by dissenting delegates and soon joined by New York governor George Clinton, former Virginia governor Patrick Henry, and others, antifederalists were organizing to stop ratification or at least to secure amendments protecting individual liberty and states' rights. By circulating their objections and proposed revisions, they hoped to encourage a coordinated response. With ratification by nine states required for the Constitution to take effect, antifederalists needed to prevail in five of the thirteen states or, for all practical purposes, any two of the big four— New York, Pennsylvania, Massachusetts, and Virginia. Whether he liked it or not, Washington would be drawn into the clash.

AMONG THE crucial states, first was Pennsylvania, whose large, unified delegation to the convention had the advantage of coming from the party that controlled the state legislature. Meeting in the same room as the Constitutional Convention and voting along party lines, that assembly called a state ratifying convention even before Congress authorized states to do so. When dissenting lawmakers attempted to forestall the vote by boycotting the session, the federalist majority dispatched the sergeant-at-arms to forcibly retrieve enough members to form a quorum. The resulting state convention acted in much the same fashion, with majority federalists ramming through ratification over opposition pleas for a less powerful presidency, more states' rights, and a bill of rights. From start to finish, the federalist case for ratification in Pennsylvania relied on public trust in Washington and Benjamin Franklin. Opponents resorted to questioning how much those men supported the Constitution and warning that while Washington could be trusted with presidential power, his successors might abuse it.

As opposition to the Constitution emerged, Washington enlisted supporters to defend it. "Much will depend," he wrote in mid-October, "on literary abilities, & the recommendation of it by good pens."[12] An October speech by the Pennsylvania delegate James Wilson so pleased Washington that he sent copies to others and urged them to distribute it widely. He did the same when the Federalist Papers, anonymously written by Hamilton, James Madison, and John Jay, began appearing. And as he came to identify more completely with the Constitution, Washington increasingly railed against its opponents. "Their objections are better calculated to alarm the fears, than to convince the judgment of readers," he complained in November. "They build them upon principles which do not exist in the Constitution—which the known & literal sense of it, does not support them in; and this too, after being flatly told that they are treading on untenable ground."[13]

Depicting the Constitution as an assault on liberty and states' rights, those antifederalists harped on the absence of a bill of rights. Federalists invariably replied that none was needed because the government would possess only enumerated powers. But those powers included sole jurisdiction over interstate commerce; control over the armed forces, foreign affairs, and matters of war and peace; authority to tax and spend for the general welfare; and all powers "necessary and proper" to carry out the enumerated ones, which, antifederalists countered, would prove virtually limitless. The Virginia delegate George Mason homed in on the president's broad authority, including the power to make treaties and appoint judges with only the Senate's assent. The Maryland delegate Luther Martin foresaw risks in empowering appointed judges to construe the Constitution as the supreme law of the land. Others carped on Congress's broad taxing powers. New Yorkers balked at constitutional limits on state import duties, while Rhode Islanders objected to the ban on state-issued paper money. To rile Virginia and the South, Henry raised the specter of a Yankee-dominated Congress abolishing slavery or limiting westward expansion. And so it went as antifederalists posited an elite conspiracy to subjugate America.

Washington closely studied these charges and found them both baseless and malicious. "To alarm the people, seems the ground work of his plan," he said of Mason in October,[14] and he soon extended these charges to antifederalists generally. "Every art that could inflame the passions and touch the interests of men has been essayed," he complained. "The ignorant have been told, that should the proposed Government obtain, their land would be taken from them and their property disposed of."[15] Their forte, Washington said of antifederalists, "seems to lie in misrepresentation" rather than a desire "to convince the understanding by some arguments."[16] He believed that liberty and property could only survive with the Constitution.

When Delaware, New Jersey, and Georgia joined Pennsylvania in ratifying the Constitution by the end of 1787, Washington began to sense victory. Despite obstacles ahead, he entered the new year both hopeful that the states would ratify the Constitution and resigned to playing his role in the new order. "I never saw him so keen for anything in my Life as he is for the adoption of this new form of Government," one guest wrote about Washington late in 1787, and as for the presidency, "I am fully of opinion he may be induced to appear once more on the Publick Stage of life."[17] Still, formidable opposition remained in the key states of Massachusetts, Virginia, and New York. Knowing their importance, Washington was willing to step up his involvement.

OF COURSE, Washington had been deeply involved in the ratification effort since returning home in September. He had personally endorsed the Constitution to public officials and influential people in Virginia and elsewhere. He had urged supporters with "literary abilities" to take up their pens on behalf of the cause and then helped to distribute the results.[18] He had never objected when federalists invoked his name and had dispatched scores of private letters of his own supporting ratification. Now, to win in Massachusetts, Madison advised Washington, more might be required of him. "I have good reason to believe that if you are in correspondence with any gentleman of that quarter, and a proper occasion offered for an explicit communication of your good wishes for the plan," Madison wrote, "that it would be attended with valuable effects."[19]

Responding to Madison's request, Washington at first demurred. "I have no regular corrispondt in Massachusetts," he wrote to Madison, "otherwise, as the occasional subject of a letter I should have had no objection to the communication of my sentiments on the proposed Government as they are unequivocal & decided."[20] Then Washington received a note seeking advice from his wartime general officer Benjamin Lincoln, who had been elected to the Massachusetts ratifying convention. Seizing the opportunity, Washington replied with a long letter intended for use at the convention endorsing the Constitution, stressing the importance of ratification by Massachusetts, and suggesting how Bay State federalists should comport themselves.

Developments in Pennsylvania colored Washington's advice. Early in the new year, reports began circulating in newspapers that a mob of unreconstructed antifederalists had disrupted a federalist victory rally in Carlisle, Pennsylvania.[21] Soon it became apparent that this riot was not an isolated event. The problems went back to the previous year, when Pennsylvania federalists had forced an early state convention and then rammed the Constitution through it without listening to the opposition. Dissenters had then collected petitions signed by thousands asking the state assembly to rescind ratification and begun working with antifederalists in other states to defeat the Constitution. Word of these developments convinced Washington that victory alone was not enough. He would have to rule these people, and he knew from the Revolutionary era that a disaffected minority could fatally disrupt public order. When the local militia freed the imprisoned rioters in Carlisle and prevented their prosecution, the lesson should have become clear to all, yet some federalists wanted the rioters and the militia punished as an example.

Washington knew better. For the new government to function, he reasoned, antifederalists would need to accept the ratification process as fundamentally fair. After initially hailing the results in Pennsylvania despite the strong-arm tactics, Washington now changed his tone. In his letter to Lincoln, Washington struck a note of conciliation. "The business of the Convention should be conducted with moderation, candor & fairness (which are not incompatible with firmness)," he wrote, "for altho' the friends of the New system may bear down the opposition yet they would never be able, by precipitate or violent measures, to soothe and reconcile their minds to the exercise of the Government." This reconciliation, Washington stressed, "is a matter that ought as much as possible to be kept in view."[22] Winning at all costs would not serve the public interest, he concluded. Whatever he thought of antifederalists, and various private letters betrayed his antipathy toward them, Washington knew better than to show it. He wanted to form an American nation by uniting its people, not dividing them.

Although Washington's letter arrived too late to influence the convention in Massachusetts, confirmation of his position reached the members from another source. Washington often wrote private letters discussing ratification. Most of these remained confidential. Key parts of one surfaced in a Virginia paper on December 27 and were reprinted in nine Massachusetts papers during the state's ratifying convention, which began on January 9, 1788. "There is *no alternative* between the *adoption* of it and *anarchy*," Washington wrote of the Constitution, "and *clear I am,* if another federal Convention is attempted, that the sentiments of its members will be *more* discordant or *less* accommodating than the last. In fine, that they will agree upon no general plan."[23] Federalists were hungry to hear such words from their icon. By March some fifty papers had reprinted key extracts from the letter. "I am fully persuaded it is the *best that can be obtained at this time,*" one of the extracts said about the Constitution, "that it is free from many of the imperfections with which it is charged, and that *it* or *disunion* is before us to choose from."[24] In one sentence Washington encapsulated the federalists' position.

The sides were so closely drawn at the Massachusetts convention that Washington's support may have been decisive. An article in the *Massachusetts Gazette* suggested as much when it observed that "the *Federalists* should be distinguished hereafter by the name of WASHINGTONIANS."[25] The outcome remained uncertain for four weeks, with both sides given every chance to make their case, until a calculated move by Governor John Hancock to adopt the antifederalists' amendments as recommendations to the first Congress instead of as conditions for ratification carried the day, 187 to 167. Adopting this approach, other states signed on over the next few months, leaving the Constitution one state shy of the nine required for ratification as Virginia, New Hampshire, and New York opened their conventions in June.

"THE PLOT THICKENS FAST," Washington wrote as Virginia's ratifying convention neared.[26] To deal with the threat posed by Henry's oratory, Washington all but ordered Madison to stand for election to the convention so that he could answer Henry point for point, a task that the reserved, scholarly Madison dreaded. When Madison's election looked doubtful, Washington told him to return from his seat in Congress to

James Madison, Pendleton's Lithography
after a portrait by Gilbert Stuart, c. 1828.
(Courtesy of Library of Congress)

stump for votes — another unpleasant task. "The consciousness
of having discharged that duty which we owe to our Country, is superior to all other considerations," Washington wrote
to Madison, his words likely reflecting his own thinking on
the presidency and certainly expressing his own strong sense
of duty.[27] Washington, of course, declined nomination to the
convention. He wished to remain above the fray and did not
want to risk being accused of acting out of self-interest — which
gave his implicit endorsement more force and would stand him
in good stead should he become president. "There will . . . be
powerful and eloquent speeches on both sides," Washington

rightly predicted for his state's convention.[28] "The Northern, or upper Counties are *generally* friendly, the lower *are said* to be generally unfriendly."[29]

Once the delegates convened in Richmond, the debate went on for weeks with neither side gaining a clear advantage. Between daily letters and newspaper reports, Washington received a blow-by-blow account of the proceedings. Though far away, he might as well have been there. "The truth was that not only at the Virginia convention but at all the state gatherings Washington was always present, a force more powerful for being insubstantial," his biographer James Thomas Flexner observed.[30] Washington's role in drafting the Constitution and the prospect of his becoming president made all the difference. Alluding to Washington near the end of Virginia's convention, the antifederalist leader William Grayson told the assembly, "Were it not for one great character in America, so many men would not be for this Government. . . . We do not fear while he lives: But we can only expect his *fame* to be immortal. We wish to know, who besides him, can concentrate the confidence and affections of all America?"[31] In making their arguments, antifederalists must have felt as though they were shadowboxing with Washington, whose assumed role as president made what they saw as a fatally flawed system appear attractive to many.

On June 27, 1788, the evening stage brought news to Alexandria that Virginia had ratified the Constitution. It had passed by a ten-vote margin at the 168-member convention. The offer of recommendatory amendments won over more delegates than expected, and concerns about frontier security tipped some states'-rights-minded delegates from Kentucky, which was then still part of Virginia but soon secured separation under the new union. With cannons booming, townspeople descended on Mount Vernon to invite Washington to festivities scheduled for the next day. Before dawn, a rider arrived with word that New Hampshire had ratified on the twenty-first, making it, not Virginia, the critical ninth state to approve the Constitution. "Thus the Citizens of Alexandria, when convened, constituted the first public company in America, which had the pleasure of pouring libation to the prosperity of the ten States that had actually adopted the general government," Washington noted.[32]

Similar celebrations took place in countless cities and towns across the country as word spread that ten states had approved the Constitution.[33] New York would not hold out for long. That state's antifederalist governor, Washington's close friend George Clinton, released his partisans at the New York convention to support ratification once news arrived that Virginia's vote had sealed the union. Victors and vanquished in both states alike recognized it as being a triumph as much for Washington as for the Constitution. "Be assured," the Virginia antifederalist leader and future president James Monroe said of Washington shortly after his state's convention ended, "his influence carried this government."[34]

These momentous events led Washington to reflect on all that Americans had achieved over the past year. "We have the unequaled privilege of choosing our own political Institutions," he wrote in August 1788, "and of improving upon the experiences of mankind in the formation of a confederated government, where due energy will not be incompatible with the unalienable rights of freemen." In a world hitherto ruled by hereditary monarchs, traditional dogmas, or military might, nothing like America's republican experiment had ever occurred. "We exhibit at present the novel & astonishing Spectacle of a whole People deliberating calmly on what form of government will be most conductive to their happiness; and deciding with an unexpected degree of unanimity in favor of a system which they conceive calculated to answer the purpose."[35]

Where before the Convention Washington had despaired of the country's survival as a free, unified republic, now he exuded confidence. "When the people shall find themselves secure under an energetic government," he wrote in mid-1788, "when foreign Nations shall be disposed to give us equal advantages in commerce from dread of retaliation, . . . and when every one (under his own vine and fig-tree) shall begin to taste the fruits of freedom — then all of these blessings (for all these blessings will come) will be referred to the fostering influence of the new government."[36] Washington could scarcely refuse to play his ordained role in that grand experiment.

WASHINGTON'S ASCENT to the presidency once the Constitution was ratified seemed to have been so foreordained as to need no explanation, but the federal election that resulted in his rise was actually more complex than many expected. It chose not only the president but also the vice president, who ran separately, and the entire Congress. It was the congressional elections that engaged Washington's attention. Even with ratification, antifederalists could strangle the new government at birth by taking over the first federal Congress.[37] Voicing this fear, Washington wrote to Madison about the opposition, "Their expedient will now probably be an attempt to procure the Election of so many of their own Junto under the New Government, as, by the introduction of local and embarrassing disputes, to impede or frustrate its operation."[38] Henry was already stumping Virginia to this end, and Clinton's party would soon do the same in New York. Still smarting from their earlier treatment, Pennsylvania antifederalists met during September to endorse a list of limiting constitutional amendments and a slate of congressional candidates who supported them and a weak federal government.

Washington left no doubt about his determination to counter this strategy by pushing for a federalist Congress. Declaring that nothing "on our part ought to be left undone," he wrote late in the summer of 1788, "I conceive it to be of unspeakable importance, that whatever there be of wisdom, & prudence, & patriotism on the Continent, should be concentrated in the public Councils, at the first outset."[39] Given the consequences at stake, he could scarcely leave himself out of the federalists' phalanx. "To be shipwrecked in sight of the Port," Washington wrote to Madison in early fall, "would be the severest of all possible aggravations to our misery."[40] At this point Washington was still publicly declaring his disinterest in the presidency and privately expressing doubts whether he would get the post if antifederalists prevailed in the elections. At some level, however, he surely wanted and expected it. Washington typically sought the center stage when significant events occurred, and as much as he loved the life of a country squire, he also enjoyed urban culture, especially when he stood at its focus. Finally, the presidency would further secure his legacy, which was always of concern to him. But everything hinged on a federalist Congress, which became his goal.

Under the original Constitution, state legislators chose senators and voters elected representatives. Thus federalists rallied to win any remaining statehouse races and as many of the congressional contests as possible. They benefited from the widely held sentiments that with the Constitution ratified, its supporters should be given the opportunity to implement it, and that Washington, as the presumptive president, should have a friendly Congress. Indeed, while his name did not appear on ballots anywhere, Washington effectively headed the federalist ticket everywhere. In Baltimore, for example, the *Maryland Journal* reported, federalists "appeared at the Polls with a Figure representing the Goddess of Federalism and an excellent Painting of General Washington." When they then won all six of the state's seats in Congress, the newspaper added the couplet, "Now all our factions, all our wars shall cease / And FED'RALS *rule* our happy land in peace."[41] The trend continued through the remaining contests, which concluded early in 1789 with federalists winning four of six sharply contested House races in Clinton's New York, giving them an overall four-to-one margin in Congress.

Senate contests produced a similar result. Federalists claimed both seats in states with federalist-controlled statehouses, such as Connecticut; antifederalists did the same in those dominated by their party, such as Virginia. The partisan rancor became so intense in New York's split legislature that it deadlocked and failed to choose anyone. Yet the overall balance favored federalists. As president, Washington would have a supportive Senate as well as a supportive House. He rejoiced in the outcome. "All the political maneuvres which were calculated to impede, if not prevent the operation of the new government, are now closed," Washington crowed upon learning that despite Henry's best efforts, federalists had won six of Virginia's ten House seats, "and although the issue of *all* the Elections are not yet known, they are sufficiently *displayed* to authorise a belief that the opposers of the government have been defeated."[42]

THE FEDERALIST SURGE further increased the clamor for Washington to become president. The Constitution's least tested and potentially most significant innovation, the presidency stood at the heart of federalists' hopes for the new union. Fearful of democracy's excesses and wary of the mob, federalists yearned for strong executive leadership. A President Washington stood as their best prospect. "No other man can sufficiently unite public opinion or can give the requisite weight to the office in the commencement of the Government," Hamilton wrote to Washington in November.[43] "No other Man can *fill* that Office," Gouverneur Morris added in December. "You alone can awe the Insolence of opposing Factions, & the greater Insolence of assuming Adherents."[44] Predicting about the presidency that "the first impressions made therein will probably give a tone to all future measures," Benjamin Lincoln appealed to Washington, "the affections of the people, and the unlimited confidence they place in your integrity and judgment, gives you an elevated stand among them which no other man can or probably ever will command." Washington's service, Lincoln assured him regarding the antifederalists, "will embarrass their Scheams if not totally baffle them."[45] Who administered the new government mattered, Morris had advised Washington, because constitutions were different in practice than they were on paper.[46]

By the end of 1788, Washington likely had come around to this point of view even though he still demurred in public and sometimes in private.[47] "It would ill become me at present to be more explicit with any person," he wrote to his farm manager about the presidency on New Year's Day 1789, but he noted in this same letter that he could only decline the office "if it may by any means be done consistently with the dictates of duty."[48] Duty would prevail, everyone who knew Washington must have known, and duty would lead him to serve.

Historians have long debated the sources of Washington's deep sense of duty. The war, some say; eighteenth-century Virginia culture, others add. Enlightenment values and religious teachings likely entered the mix, as did being the first child born to a strong-willed mother. Washington always yearned to leave a legacy, and the lack of any children of his own, even one to inherit Mount Vernon, may have mattered. "You will become the Father to more than three Millions of Children," Morris wrote to Washington about the presidency in a well-aimed plea.[49] Further, Washington's sense of duty was tied to his belief in Providence and a divinely ordained mission.

During the Revolutionary War, Washington had come to believe that American independence was ordained by God and that he was fated to play a part in achieving it. His near miraculous preservation in battle reinforced this sense. When the war ended, he initially saw his life's mission as fulfilled and brooded on death. But he gradually came to see a further purpose for himself in forging a new union that would safeguard American liberty and ultimately in serving as the nation's first president.

Over the course of 1788 Washington had articulated three main goals for the United States under the Constitution: respect abroad, prosperity at home, and development westward.[50] Toward these ends, he envisioned a vigorous federal government encouraging trade, manufacturing, and agriculture through effective tariffs, sound money, secure property rights, and a nonaligned foreign policy. "America under an efficient government, will be the most favorable Country of any in the world for persons of industry and frugality," Washington asserted in mid-1788, and "not be less advantageous to the happiness of the lowest class of people because of . . . the great plenty of unoccupied land."[51] Indeed, in a world dominated by authoritarian regimes where the many served the few, he saw it as a model for individual liberty and republican rule everywhere.

ALTHOUGH NOT EXPLICITLY designed to lift Washington to the presidency, the original electoral-vote system served that purpose. Under it, Washington need not seek a party's nomination or campaign for votes. He was not even required to put himself forward for the office. Electors were selected independently in each state either by voters or by the legislature and then cast their two votes. By this point, faction mattered most in their selection: were they for or against the Constitution?

Virtually everyone predicted that Washington would sweep

the race by receiving one vote from each elector regardless of the elector's stance on the Constitution. Federalists effectively controlled the government in every participating state except Virginia and New York, and Washington surely would win in those too. Even if he wanted to, Patrick Henry could not deny Washington in his home state; and even if he could, George Clinton would not want to deny his old friend in New York.[52] Antifederalists focused instead on how to elect Clinton as vice president, while federalists struggled to coalesce around John Adams. In the end, while every elector voted for Washington, enough scattered their second vote that Adams did not even receive votes from a majority of them. He did get more than anyone else, though, which was enough to claim the crown as America's Prince of Wales, as he once called himself as vice president. Clinton would have to wait sixteen years for that prize.

By the end of 1788 Washington was confident enough of the election's outcome to ask David Humphreys to draft a presidential inaugural address for him. What remains of the seventy-three-page speech, though never delivered, provides a window into Washington's thoughts as he approached the presidency. The General and his trusted aide, then a houseguest at Mount Vernon, likely worked closely together on the draft, with Humphreys serving as something between a scribe and a ghostwriter for his former boss. Indeed, Washington made Humphreys's draft his own by copying it in his own hand, perhaps revising as he went. He then sent a copy for comment to Madison, also a trusted adviser, who deemed it too long, too specific, and too politically indiscreet.

In laying out his vision for the new government, the draft showed how broadly Washington interpreted the Constitution and how fully he intended to use it to create a nation out of the several states and territories. Three decades later, the first editor of Washington's papers, Jared Sparks, after deciding with Madison's approval to destroy the only copy, cut it into pieces for souvenir hunters seeking samples of the General's handwriting. Madison by that time had moved away from his earlier ardent nationalism to found and later lead a party that welcomed antifederalists into its fold. Surviving parts of this magisterial address make up less than half of the whole. Historians treasure the remainder as authoritative: it articulated Washington's nationalist vision for the United States.[53]

Washington's draft inaugural began by denouncing the Articles of Confederation for giving the central government too little power and by embracing the Constitution for greatly expanding central authority. "No other or greater powers appear to me to be delegated to this government than are essential to accomplish the objects for which it was instituted, to wit, the safety & happiness of the governed," the address declared in a direct refutation of antifederalist claims to the contrary. And in a world of self-justifying monarchies, the stated goal of serving the people's interests signaled a sea change for government. "I rejoice in the belief," the new president was to say, "that mankind will reverse the absurd position that *the many* were made for *the few;* and that they will not continue slaves in one part of the globe, when they can become freemen in another." Toward this end, the speech exclaimed, America would play a part, "the salutary consequences of which shall flow to another Hemisphere & extend throughout the interminable series of ages!"[54] Washington never made a clearer proclamation of what made the United States special.

Republican rule founded on secure institutions stood at the heart of Washington's vision for an American empire destined to grow through free immigration and western expansion rather than at the expense of other nations. "This Constitution is really in its formation a government of the people; that is to say, a government in which all power is derived from, and at stated periods reverts to them," his address declared, and "the balances, arising from the distribution of the Legislative, Executive, and Judicial powers are the best that have been instituted." Given the Constitution's prospects for advancing republican ideals, Washington's address urged Congress and the states not to amend it until after "a fair experiment of its effects," except perhaps to add a bill of rights. Instead, Congress should "take measures for promoting the general welfare" by utilizing the powers afforded it under the Constitution to regulate coinage and currency, set just weights and measures, improve education and manners, boost arts and sciences, enhance postal services, provide patents for useful inventions, and cherish institutions favorable to humanity.[55] More than simply articulating Washington's vision for America, this draft speech outlined in advance the main features of his remarkable presidency.

With the election over, it only remained for Congress to count the electoral votes and call Washington to the seat of government in New York. This happened in April 1789, with Congress then dispatching its longtime secretary, Charles Thomson, to deliver the news. "You are called not only by the unanimous votes of the Electors but by the voice of America," Thomson informed the General at Mount Vernon.[56] Knowing that his words would reach a national audience, Washington replied from a prepared text. "I have been long accustomed to entertain so great a respect for the opinion of my fellow citizens, that the knowledge of their unanimous suffrages having been given in my favour scarcely leaves me the alternative for an Option," he said. Washington would do his duty. Then to Thomson he added, "I shall therefore be in readiness to set out the day after to morrow, and shall be happy in the pleasure of your company."[57] They traveled with Humphreys in

Washington's closed carriage with three or four liveried slaves perched outside.[58] Without prior planning or advance staging, the spontaneous outpouring of the American people transformed this simple trip into a grand public procession that helped to launch a nation.

CHAPTER FIVE

The Coronation

1789

ABOUT TEN O'CLOCK I bade adieu to Mount Vernon, to private life, and to domestic felicity; and . . . set out for New York in the company of Mr. Thomson and colonel Humphreys," Washington wrote in his diary entry for April 16, 1789.[1] His wife, Martha, remained at home with her grandchildren until suitable accommodations could be arranged in New York. She had no idea what she would miss and likely would have gone along had she known. She enjoyed a party nearly as much as her husband did, and the movable festivities that ensued were beyond any American's experience or expectations.

Washington and his traveling companions did not travel alone for long. A crowd of Virginians met them outside Mount Vernon and led Washington to Alexandria for a midday reception. "Again your country demands your care," the mayor proclaimed. "Go; and make a grateful people happy." Echoing the theme of national unity, which resonated throughout his trip, Washington replied that despite his "love" of retirement, "an ardent desire, on my own part, to be instrumental in conciliating the good will of my countrymen towards each other" had induced him to accept the presidency. After an early dinner with those he called "my affectionate friends and kind neighbors," Washington left Virginia about 2:00 p.m. aboard the Potomac River ferry.[2]

Not to be outdone by the Virginians, a sea of Marylanders hailing him as *their* president waited at the Georgetown landing for the ferry to arrive. Hundreds of these well-wishers escorted Washington as far as Spurrier's Tavern, near Bladensburg, on the post road to Baltimore. There he spent the night. With Washington assuming the office, the presidency was already serving as a source for American identity. Neither reception had been formally planned, nor had anyone told Washington about them in advance. They were spontaneous outpourings of popular sentiment. No one, it seemed, wanted to miss the occasion.

Crowds grew as Washington advanced into the more densely populated middle states. "This great man was met some miles from Town, by a large body of respectable citizens on horseback, and conducted, under a discharge of cannon . . . through crowds of admiring spectators," a report from Baltimore noted.[3] Without official authorization or prodding from the state or city government, a committee of merchants and former army officers had organized this rousing reception in what was then America's fifth largest city. The committee called on "citizens of the United States" to venerate their president, and their welcoming address declared, "We behold a new era springing out of our independence."[4] Then or the night before, Washington received a long poetic tribute that closed with the plea,

> The Federal Union closer bind,
>   Firm public faith restore;
> Drive discord from the canker'd mind,
>   Each mutual blessing pour.[5]

After spending the night of April 17 in Baltimore and getting a late start because of the ongoing receptions and festivities, Washington only got as far as Harford, Maryland, the next day. Leaving Harford early on the nineteenth, the presidential party crossed the Susquehanna River at Havre de Grace and was greeted warmly at Elkton before reaching Delaware in the afternoon.

The scene in Maryland was repeated in Delaware, where local citizens massed at the state line to meet Washington on April 19 and escorted him to Wilmington for the night. Another crowd, this one with a military escort, ushered him as far as the Pennsylvania border early on the twentieth.[6] There, with the portraitist of the American Revolution and Philadelphia impresario Charles Willson Peale orchestrating events on behalf of an official committee, celebrations topped anything Washington's party had yet encountered.

The Pennsylvania state president, Thomas Mifflin, greeted Washington at the Pennsylvania line and along with other officials, two cavalry units, a detachment of artillery, and a body of light infantry accompanied him toward Philadelphia. After a brief stop for a late breakfast in Chester, Washington left his carriage and mounted a richly ornamented white horse to lead the procession, which grew as more troops and citizens joined it along the way. Cedar and laurel branches lined the bridge across the Schuylkill River at Gray's Ferry, with evergreen arches covering each end. As Washington passed under the first triumphal arch, Peale's daughter Angelica, hidden in the branches, lowered a laurel wreath onto or just above his head.[7]

Philadelphia exploded upon Washington's arrival. Cannons fired and bells rang throughout the day; fireworks lit the night's sky. "The number of spectators who filled the doors, windows, and streets, which he passed, was greater than on any other occasion," a newspaper noted, greater even than the city's population. "All classes and descriptions of citizens discovered . . . the most undisguised attachment and unbounded zeal for their dear chief."[8] No one summoned members of this crowd; they came on their own. A formal banquet with invited guests followed at City Tavern, beginning with a toast to "The United States" and ending with one to "Liberty without licentiousness."[9] After spending one night at the

Washington's 1789 inaugural journey, prepared under the author's direction by Richard H. Britton, mapmaker, for the Fred W. Smith Presidential Library for the Study of George Washington. (Used by permission of the Mount Vernon Ladies' Association)

palatial mansion of his old friend Robert Morris, where he received more official tributes in the morning, Washington left the city at 10:00 a.m. on April 21 cheered on by another spontaneous public outpouring of affection and support.[10]

After traveling north along the Delaware River for thirty miles in Pennsylvania, Washington took a commercial ferry across to New Jersey. This passage occurred at the narrows where Washington and his army had crossed in rowboats on that fateful Christmas night in 1776 to surprise the Hessian troops at Trenton and reverse the course of the Revolutionary War. Now, however, a vast throng of state residents—male and female, young and old—lined the far side to hail Washington's return with such loud, spontaneous huzzas that, according to one observer, "the shores reecho the cheerful sounds."[11]

Local units of the New Jersey militia then preceded Washington, again on horseback, to the old stone bridge over Assunpink Creek, just south of Trenton, where his army had held off British troops on January 2, 1777. A hastily built floral arch now spanned the bridge, with laurel-entwined pillars and a banner reading "The Defender of the Mothers, will be the Protector of the Daughters."[12] Led by some of those mothers defended by his army in 1777, white-robed daughters to be protected by his presidency serenaded Washington at the arch:

Virgins fair, and Matron grave,
Those thy conquering Arms did save,
Build for thee triumphal Bowers.
Strew, ye Fair, his Way with Flowers.[13]

At the last line, the girls scattered petals along Washington's path. "The scene was truly grand," one newspaper observed of this artfully planned reception, and the sentiments it evoked "bathed many cheeks with tears."[14] From the Assunpink Bridge, Washington rode into Trenton on horseback for dinner

George Washington Entering Trenton 1789,
by Kurz & Allison, 1907.
(Courtesy of Library of Congress)

and a public reception, then on to another reception in Princeton. Washington slept there. On April 22 he traveled with a
military escort to New Brunswick for an early afternoon public
banquet and finally to Woodbridge, New Jersey, for the night.

WITH WOODBRIDGE, Washington had reached the penul-
timate stop on the week-long journey to his inauguration in
New York. It only remained for him to descend to the dock
at Elizabethtown early the morning of April 23 and cross the
Hudson River to Manhattan. The astonishing and largely
spontaneous popular reception that he received along the way
reflected his celebrated status as a war hero, of course, but
something more significant was afoot. It was a celebration of
nationhood. Washington had twice passed through much of

the same territory in 1787 without much fanfare. The banner at Trenton had said it all: once the defender in war, now the protector in peace. And as Americans are an ever forward-looking people, the hope of future protection likely meant more to them than the memory of past defense. Just as Washington had once led the Revolutionary army that defended the previous generation, Washington would now lead the government that would protect the next one, and that mattered to them.

In acclaiming Washington on his inaugural journey, Americans were cheering more than a celebrity passing through their towns. They were celebrating the nation that they had created through their elected representatives to state ratifying conventions and the president whom they had chosen through their electors. All of this was utterly unprecedented. They were not hailing a heredity monarch imposed on them by the grace of God or an accident of birth. They applauded their own elected leader and their nation, which he represented. This second American revolution, the one resulting in the ratified Constitution, was as much a popular one as the first, which had secured the country's independence. In a sense, by turning out in such large numbers to greet Washington on this occasion, they were participating in that revolution's closing act.

Buoyed by his reception, Washington rose early on April 23 and was on his way shortly after sunrise. By 9:00 a.m. he had completed the nine-mile carriage ride from Woodbridge to Elizabethtown, on the Hudson River's western bank, where an official delegation and cheering throng escorted him aboard a purposely built barge for the passage to New York. "She is 47 feet keel," one newspaper reported of the barge, "and rows with 13 oars on each side, to be manned by pilots of New-York, who are to be dressed in white frocks and black caps, trimmed and ornamented with fringe."[15] Fit for a king or perhaps a pharaoh—another paper likened it to "Cleopatra's silken-corded barge"—the craft had a canopied pavilion with festooned red curtains.[16] Although short, this was no ordinary voyage.

Seven members of Congress and three New York officials joined Washington on the barge, which gathered a flotilla of boats in its wake, including two with choirs and one bearing Henry Knox, John Jay, and other federal officers. Ships in the harbor and batteries on shore fired their guns in salute as the barge rounded Manhattan Island heading for Murray's Landing on the East River at the foot of Wall Street. Pulling alongside, one of the floating choirs sang its version of "God Save the King":

> These shores a HEAD shall own,
> Unsully'd by a throne,
> Our much lov'd WASHINGTON,
> The Great, the Good![17]

"We now discovered the Shores crowded with thousands of people," one passenger on board wrote about the barge's approach to Manhattan. "You could see little else along the Shores, in the Streets, and on Board every Vessel, but Heads standing as thick as Ears of Corn before Harvest."[18] The crowd did not comprise just New Yorkers: thousands had poured into the city from the surrounding countryside and neighboring states for the occasion. Governor Clinton warmly greeted his old friend at the Landing and walked with him, other officials, a military honor guard, and two bands through a crush of well-wishers to the residence rented by Congress for the president about a half-mile away. They finally arrived there about three hours after noon. The near universal response to the jubilation was, as one newspaper reported it, "Well, he deserves it all!"[19] Again, the nation was being feted as much as its elected leader. Clinton's presence made it all but universal.

With Washington as president, even the country's leading anti-federalist joined the celebration of nationhood. The two men dined together that night.

EVEN AS NEW YORKERS added to the prestige of the presidency by cheering Washington's entrance into their city, John Adams displayed a misunderstanding of the foundations for power in a republic by futilely trying to impose authority on the office by fiat. Installed as vice president and the Senate's presiding officer two days earlier, as Washington entered the city Adams was lecturing the Senate about the imperative of giving the president an imperial title. He wanted something like "his Most Benign Highness" or "your Majesty," it turned out, and dismissed the mere designation "President" as something suited to the chief officer of a cricket club or a fire company. America's chief executive must have a title equal to that of European royalty or he would lose respect at home and abroad, Adams argued, and one superior to the "your Excellency" commonly afforded state governors or the relative place of the central government in the federal scheme would slip and anarchy would result. Further, he claimed, titles would attract people to serve in government, and he sought a similar or the same one for his office too.[20]

At the time, Congress still had not yet fixed when, where, and how to inaugurate the president. On a motion made by Adams himself, which a vice president could then do, on April 23 the Senate named a committee to consider this pressing issue as well as the titles to be conferred on the president and the vice president.[21] Opposition to the second matter quickly surfaced. Privately calling it "truly ridiculous," the Pennsylvania senator William Maclay tried to delete consideration of titles from the committee's charge.[22] He later blamed "this Whole silly Business" mostly on Adams. No title could possibly "add to the

respect entertained for General Washington," Maclay maintained.[23] Rather than gaining respect by becoming president,
Washington gave respect to the presidency by holding it. With
the Virginia congressman James Madison taking the lead and
Washington in full accord, the House of Representatives refused to confer any supplementary title on the president. Aware
that everything he did in office set precedent, Washington an-
swered to "Mr. President," though most old friends and former
army comrades continued to call him "General."

Dodging the controversial issue of executive titles, on
April 25 the House and the Senate agreed on the time, place,
and manner for inaugurating the president. With Washington's assent, they set the date for April 30 and asked the highest
available judicial officer, New York's chancellor Robert Livingston, to administer the oath of office.[24] By then, sixty-seven of
Congress's seventy-nine members had reached New York and
taken their seats. Both houses initially agreed to stage the event
inside Federal Hall's first-floor House chamber, which (while
larger than the second-floor Senate chamber) would have limited the audience to invited guests.

Then the members had a brilliant idea. "To the end that
the oath of office may be administered to the President in the
most public manner, and that the greatest number of people
of the United States, and *without distinction,* may be witnesses
to solemnity," the *New-York Daily Gazette* reported, Congress
switched the venue for the swearing-in ceremony to "the outer
gallery adjoining to the senate-chamber."[25] This put the event
outside, on a balcony overlooking the wide intersection of Wall
and Broad Streets. At the urging of local clergy, Congress also
added that after the inauguration the official party would go to
the Episcopal Church's stately St. Paul's Chapel, on Broadway,
for public prayers led by the congressional chaplain.[26] By moving the inauguration outside, where thousands could watch,

and scheduling public prayers for the new president in a large local church, Congress implicitly recognized the remarkable popular response to Washington's becoming president. More than Congress, the presidency was becoming the publicly recognized symbol of the constitutional union, and by reaching out to the public as he did during his journey to New York, Washington further helped to forge a nation.

Countless individual spectators who witnessed Washington's journey to New York or were in the city for his inauguration spoke in almost breathless wonder about the moment when they seemed to catch his eye or he appeared to doff his hat or bow to them alone.[27] In Europe, all Americans knew, people bowed to kings. On his journey and in New York, Washington continually bowed to people as his way of acknowledging tributes and cheers. It endeared him to them. Perhaps to compensate for his poor public speaking, which was aggravated by his false teeth, Washington became a master of the correct gesture. As in Newburgh, when donning his reading glasses helped to carry the day after his speech failed to persuade, so a nod or a glance or a bow by Washington could command an audience or seal a deal. Many successful American presidents would have this ability, but none more than Washington.

Perhaps because he lacked such an ability, Adams missed this point, as evidenced by his desire to separate the people from the president by interposing regal titles. "The glare of royalty and nobility, during his mission to England, had made him believe their fascination a necessary ingredient to government," Thomas Jefferson later wrote about Adams, but Washington knew better.[28] The American experience, he had noted in his undelivered inaugural address, reversed the presumption that "the many were made for the few" by establishing that government was made for the many.[29] Washington would replicate his jubilant journey to New York with trips through New

England and the South over the next two years, making it his goal as president to visit every state. Further, while in office, he regularly received the public at his residence.[30] Although Washington was not an informal man, his became an open presidency, quite unlike the insulated monarchies of Europe.[31] Indeed, within a few weeks Madison observed that because of Washington's performance in it, the presidency was the only feature of the new government that had captured the popular imagination.[32]

In his diary entry for the day of his triumphal entry into New York, Washington wrote that while he found the pageantry pleasing, "considering the reverse of this scene, which may be the case after all my labors do no good," he also found it painful.[33] Expanding on this point in a letter written two weeks later to South Carolina's Edward Rutledge, Washington cautioned about the cheering crowds, "I fear if the issue of the public measures should not corrispond with their sanguine expectation, they will turn the extravagant (and I may say undue) praises which they are heaping upon me at this moment, into equally extravagant (though I will fondly hope unmerited) censures."[34]

Washington saw public opinion as a formidable but fickle foundation for political power and tried to cultivate it. His evident success led the less popular Adams, with a mixture of esteem and envy, to view Washington somewhat as an actor playing a part: a "Character of Convention," Adams called him, designedly made "popular and fashionable with all parties and in all places and with all persons as a center of union" first during the war and again as president.[35] Indeed, Adams later called Washington the finest political actor he had ever seen, and those public displays helped to cement the union with the presidency at its head.

WITH CONGRESS scheduling his inauguration for the last day of April, Washington had a week to settle in before becoming president. Upon his arrival in New York, he dined at the governor's mansion, but thereafter he let people know that he would not accept any further dinner invitations, and so he received none.[36] He took his meals at the presidential residence with his closest aides, Tobias Lear and David Humphreys.[37] There, the president-elect also received visitors. From "the time I had done breakfast, thence 'till dinner, & afterwards 'till bed time," he noted about these days between his arrival and the inaugural, "I could not dispatch one ceremonius visit before I was called to another—so that in fact I had no leizure to read, or answer the dispatches which were pouring in from all quarters."[38]

Many accounts had Washington conferring often with Madison during this period on matters of state and the inaugural address.[39] Meanwhile, Congress worked mostly on raising revenue and establishing courts. By April 30, if not before, Washington had a brief new inaugural address in hand and was ready to take office. With people streaming into New York to watch the ceremonies, local, state, and federal officials hurriedly organized the various events. "We have heard much of the BIRTH DAY of our COLUMBIA," New York's *Gazette of the United States* proclaimed in large type on April 29. "TO MORROW is the Day of her ESPOUSALS—when, in presence of the KING of KINGS, the solemn Compact will be ratified between her, and the darling object of her choice." Washington, the paper exclaimed, by "UNIVERSAL SUFFRAGES OF A GREAT AND VARIOUS PEOPLE" would become president.[40]

That much-awaited day began with a cannon volley at sunrise followed by church bells ringing throughout the morning. Crowds gathered in front of the president's house, but

Washington remained inside until a deputation from the Senate and the House arrived shortly after noon to report that Congress was ready to receive him. The retired general wore a tailed suit of brown Connecticut broadcloth with American-eagle buttons and tight, calf-length pants; white, knee-high silk stockings; and silver-buckle shoes. A hat, powdered hair, and dress sword completed his inaugural costume. Stepping outside, Washington bowed to the crowd before boarding a state coach. His own carriage, with Humphreys and Lear on board, waited behind the presidential coach as troops and dignitaries arrayed themselves in a preset order. At 12:30 p.m. the parade began moving slowly south on Cherry to Queen Street, then around to Broad Street before swinging north toward the stately, recently restored and renamed Federal Hall, where Washington would take the oath of office prescribed in the Constitution.

One company of cavalry and three of infantry, about five hundred soldiers in all, led the procession through cheering crowds from the presidential residence onward. The delegation from Congress followed the troops, then came Washington, his two aides, heads of the federal departments, Chancellor Livingston, and other invited dignitaries. Citizens fell in behind the official party as it passed, all winding their way toward Federal Hall. "About two hundred yards before reaching the hall," wrote the popular American author Washington Irving, who witnessed the event as a child, "Washington and his suite alighted from their carriages and passed through the troops, who were drawn up on each side, into the hall and senate chamber, where the Vice-President, the Senate and House of Representatives were assembled."[41]

The senators, who had assembled in their chamber first, at the vice president's prodding discussed whether they should stand or sit while the president spoke. The underlying issue, debated now on the fly, involved the weighty matter of whether members of Congress were equal, superior, or inferior to the president. Adams and Senators Richard Henry Lee and Ralph Izard related their personal observations of the king addressing Parliament, but others dismissed those comments as of "no consequence" in a republic. Before the Senate settled anything, however, House members filed in behind their Speaker and took seats to the senators' right. More than an hour more passed before Washington finally reached the chamber, walked between the now standing members, bowed to each side, and took a seat on the dais between the vice president and the Speaker. Then the members sat. Lacking any clear instruction on protocol, the members tended to stand and sit along with the president, suggesting a rough sort of respectful equality between the branches.[42]

Soon after Washington sat down, Adams stood up to invite him onto the Senate's outer gallery to take the oath of office. Thousands were waiting to watch.[43] "The windows and the roofs of the houses were crowded," Eliza Morton observed from atop one of those roofs, "and in the streets the throng was so dense that it seemed as if one might literally walk on the heads of the people."[44] Washington stepped outside first, followed by Adams, Livingston, and as many of the assembled dignitaries and members of Congress as would fit. The only known live drawing of the event, a sketch by Peter Lecour turned into a print in 1790, shows eighteen people crammed on the narrow porch with Washington. Decades later, Morton could still recall the "universal shouts of joy and welcome" that greeted Washington's appearance on the gallery.[45]

Placing his hand on the large, red Bible fetched for the occasion from Livingston's Masonic Lodge, Washington repeated the oath administered by the chancellor precisely as set forth in the Constitution. Contrary to later accounts, contemporary

Detail from *Federal Hall,* re-engraved by Sidney L. Smith after
a print by Amos Doolittle of a drawing by Peter Lecour, 1899.
(Courtesy of Library of Congress)

ones suggest that Washington did not add the words "so help
me God" to the prescribed oath but, master of the gesture, did
lean over and kiss the Bible. In the crammed streets far below,
no spectator would have heard the added words anyway, while
most could see the gesture. Indeed, few of them heard anything said from the balcony until the end, when Livingston
proclaimed in a loud voice, "Long live George Washington,
President of the United States!"[46] Then they erupted again,
cannons fired, and church bells rang.

PRESIDENT WASHINGTON, after bowing to the people, went
back into the Senate chamber to address Congress and invited

guests — perhaps a hundred persons in all. The audience for this speech, however, was much larger than Congress. Newspapers across America printed it, and foreign ministers in attendance reported on it to Europe. By substituting the short, general inaugural address crafted by Madison for the long, specific one prepared with Humphreys, Washington chose to reveal little about his policy objectives or his incoming administration. The historian Joseph Ellis has described the speech as "deliberately elliptical."[47] It gave no hint of the nation-building efforts Washington's administration would pursue, particularly after Alexander Hamilton replaced Madison as the president's closest adviser, even though that basic course of action flowed logically from much that Washington had expressed at least privately and often publicly since his Circular Letter of 1783. It did not even disclose much about Washington beyond his faith in Divine Providence.

While Washington had "the Gift of Silence," as Adams once put it, and could command an audience with his gestures, he was not a natural orator and never owned this speech.[48] Still, delivered in a mumble that people strained to hear, the address had a quiet dignity. The Spanish minister called it "eloquent and appropriate" even if the presentation struck some as "ungainly."[49] Six paragraphs long, the speech began with the president noting his "incapacity as well as disinclination for the weighty and untried cares before me." Then, after expressing his trust in God and Congress to carry the government forward, Washington reminded Americans of their national purpose. "The preservation of the sacred fire of liberty," he stated, "and the destiny of the republican model of Government, are justly considered as deeply, perhaps as finally, staked, on the experiment entrusted to the hands of the American people." Turning to the widely discussed issue of amending the Constitution, after urging Congress to "avoid every alteration which

might endanger the benefits of an united and effective government," Washington endorsed additions that might "more
impregnably fortif[y]" the "rights of freemen." By this turn of
phrase, he backed a bill of rights for some while artfully dodging both the already pressing subject of slavery and the then
more remote topic of women's rights. Looking heavenward, he
closed his address by asking divine blessing for "the enlarged
views, the temperate consultations, and the wise measures, on
which the success of this Government must depend."[50]

Reading with some hesitation from pages that he shifted
awkwardly from hand to hand, Washington took twenty minutes to deliver the fourteen-hundred-word address. From his
entrance to his exit, the ceremony at Federal Hall ran under
an hour. Thousands waited outside for the resumption of the
inaugural parade, which the whole Congress now joined. Led
by the same troops and assembled in a similar order as during
the procession to Federal Hall, the augmented official party
now walked several blocks up Broadway to St. Paul's Chapel,
which it entered for divine services. More than five years earlier, Washington and his troops had paraded down this same
wide avenue after liberating New York at the end of the Revolutionary War. Although the city's population had increased
dramatically since the war, many of the people hailing Washington on this late April afternoon had done so in 1783. Now
even more than then, he personified the nation that was taking
shape around them.

The church service did not last long. The Episcopal bishop
Samuel Provoost, who also served as the Senate's chaplain, led
prayers and sang praises but did not deliver a sermon. After
the service, Washington rode by coach to his residence in time
for a private dinner before going out at dusk with Humphreys
and Lear to watch fireworks from Livingston's house, which
overlooked the harbor.[51] So many people packed the streets of

lower Manhattan during and after the fireworks that coaches could not pass. Washington chose to walk home. That night he had much to see. At the urging of civic leaders, New Yorkers celebrated the inauguration by illuminating the city with arrays of candles and lanterns in street-facing windows, front doors, open spaces, and public buildings. The most elaborate displays added transparencies that cast images fit for the occasion. In some, Washington could see himself, his victories, or his virtues; in others, he saw the nation's shape or symbols. Washington and the United States were the two themes on display that night, and in some of the illuminations, they overlapped or blurred together.

After walking north for nearly a mile through thinning crowds and darkening neighborhoods, Washington reached the presidential residence after 10:00 p.m. and retired for the night. "It was a day which will stand immutable and indelebale in the Annals of America," Lear wrote in a letter to Mount Vernon urging the president's wife to come soon.[52] "Good government, the best of blessings, now commences under favorable auspices," the next day's newspaper announced. "We beg to congratulate our readers on the great event."[53] Those readers and all Americans arose that morning, May 1, 1789, to the first full day of the first federal administration.

THAT NEW ADMINISTRATION did much to institutionalize the federalists' nationalistic vision for America. As with drafting the Constitution and orchestrating its ratification, Washington never worked alone in this effort or deserved exclusive credit for it. Instinctively he leaned toward cabinet government, a feature of the American political system never explicitly prescribed in the Constitution but one that became established through Washington's practice. In accord with his wartime leadership style, this structure for the American executive branch allowed Washington to listen to the advice of officers in council and made it easier for him to delegate authority, assign responsibility, and share recognition. As the wise and witty future High Federalist senator from New York, Gouverneur Morris, had counseled Washington shortly after the Philadelphia Convention, constitutions take life by use and are never the same on paper as in practice.[54] From his first day in office to his retirement eight years later, Washington and his cabinet brought the Constitution to life.

Building a national market economy took precedence, with Hamilton playing a key role as Washington's treasury secretary. Under the confederation, some rich states had all but taken over the domestic war debt, and some poor ones had undermined property rights by excessively printing unsecured paper money. Both policies had undermined the union. Hamilton's nationalizing program started with having the central government fund the full war debt owed by Congress and the states. He viewed this as a means to align the interests of wealthy Americans with those of the nation, displace the states as independent economic actors, and enhance the central government's credit. To pay for it, Hamilton pushed a tariff on imported goods, which had the side-effect of sheltering American industry, and an excise tax on some domestic items such as whiskey, which he saw as a means to exert central authority over frontier distillers. As a capstone for his economic program, Hamilton gained Washington's support for a controversial central bank for the United States, which served to regulate fiscal policy, provide a stable national currency, and reduce the state's role in monetary matters.

Washington had other concerns for the new nation. Working with Knox as secretary of war and Jefferson as secretary of state, Washington doggedly pursued his frontier vision to open the Ohio country for settlement, leading to prolonged warfare with the Western Confederacy, an alliance of native tribes, until its capitulation in 1795. Jay pitched in by negotiating a treaty that, along with less popular provisions, finally secured the assent of Britain to leave its forts in the Northwest Territory. Two western states, Tennessee and Kentucky, joined the union, as did Vermont and the two original states that had not previously ratified the Constitution, North Carolina and Rhode Island. With surprisingly little dissent after all the opposition the idea had generated at the Constitutional Convention, Congress authorized a network of lower federal courts that projected central authority into every state. With Washington's support, Madison pushed a bill of rights through an indifferent, federalist-dominated Congress. Jefferson made further contributions to the emerging national order by devising a broad regime of federally protected intellectual property rights and, in a compromise with Hamilton, moving the seat of government to a projected new federal city near Washington's Mount Vernon. By the end of his second term, as Washington oversaw planning for the city that would bear his name, he could see much of his national vision being realized.

Washington suffered disappointments as well. He fell out with Jefferson and Madison during his second term as they turned against Hamilton's national bank and Jay's treaty with Britain. Increasingly, they linked with former antifederalists to form first an opposition caucus in Congress and ultimately a formal national political party with a states'-rights bent. Organizing on the left led to organizing on the right, resulting in two ideologically distinct parties that instinctively took opposite sides on policy issues. The resulting partisanship pained Washington, who believed in consensus government. The excesses of the French Revolution and the cataclysmic European wars those disturbances had spawned complicated Washington's effort to maintain a nonaligned foreign policy that kept the United States at peace and trading with all countries.

Two terms proved enough for Washington. He had wanted to retire even earlier. His 1796 farewell address to the American people, a widely read document that he never delivered in person, warned them "against the baneful effects of the spirit of party" and urged them "to steer clear of permanent alliances with any portion of the foreign world." Nationalism remained his main theme, however, as he admonished them, using capital letters for emphasis, "The name of AMERICAN, which belongs to you in your national capacity, must always exalt the just pride of patriotism, more than any appellation derived from local discriminations."[55] For him, that meant that being an American took precedent over being a Virginian.

Dying at age sixty-seven, less than three years after retiring from the presidency, Washington did not live to see the nineteenth century. It was during that century, however, that the ideals he championed became firmly established at home and began spreading abroad. Liberty, representative government, and nationalism increasingly became global watchwords and rallying cries for people everywhere. They were never Washington's ideas alone. He had learned them from the American people as much as they had learned them from him. Each had wider sources as well, and wider impact. By helping to forge a nation on American ideals, Washington became a citizen of the world.

NOTES

Abbreviations for Frequently Cited Works

Annals of Congress   *The Debates and Proceedings in the Congress of the United States.* 42 vols. Washington, DC: Gales & Seaton, 1834.

DGW   Donald Jackson and Dorothy Twohig, eds. *The Diaries of George Washington.* 6 vols. Charlottesville: University Press of Virginia, 1976–79.

DHFFC   Linda Grant DePauw et al., eds. *The Documentary History of the First Federal Congress of the United States of America.* 15 vols. Baltimore: Johns Hopkins University Press, 1972–.

DHFFE   Merrill Jensen et al., eds. *The Documentary History of the First Federal Election.* 4 vols. Madison: University of Wisconsin Press, 1976–89.

DHRC   Merrill Jensen et al., eds. *The Documentary History of the Ratification of the Constitution.* 26 vols. Madison: State Historical Society of Wisconsin, 1976–.

Farrand   Max Farrand, ed. *The Record of the Federal Convention of 1787.* Rev. ed. 4 vols. New Haven, CT: Yale University Press, 1937.

GWD   John C. Fitzpatrick, ed. *The Diaries of George Washington, 1748–1799.* 4 vols. Boston: Houghton Mifflin, 1925.

JCC   Library of Congress. *Journals of the Continental Congress, 1774–1789.* 34 vols. Washington, DC: Government Printing Office, 1904–37.

PAH   Harold C. Syrett and Jacob Cooke, eds. *The Papers of Alexander Hamilton.* 27 vols. New York: Columbia University Press, 1961–87.

PGM   Robert A. Rutland, ed. *The Papers of George Mason, 1725–1792.* 3 vols. Chapel Hill: University of North Carolina Press, 1970.

PGW, CS   W. W. Abbot et al., eds. *The Papers of George Washington: Confederation Series.* 6 vols. Charlottesville: University Press of Virginia, 1992–97.

PGW, PS   W. W. Abbot et al., eds. *The Papers of George Washington: Presidential Series.* 16 vols. Charlottesville: University Press of Virginia, 1987–.

PGW, RS   Dorothy Twohig et al., eds. *The Papers of George Washington: Retirement Series.* 4 vols. Charlottesville: University Press of Virginia, 1998–99.

PGW, RWS   W. W. Abbot et al., eds. *The Papers of George Washington: Revolutionary War Series.* 22 vols. Charlottesville: University Press of Virginia, 1985–.

PJM   Robert A. Rutland et al., eds. *The Papers of James Madison.* 17 vols. Chicago: University of Chicago Press; Charlottesville: University Press of Virginia, 1962–.

PTJ   Julian P. Boyd et al., eds. *The Papers of Thomas Jefferson.* 39 vols. Princeton, NJ: Princeton University Press, 1950–.

WGW   John Clement Fitzpatrick, ed. *The Writings of George Washington from the Original Manuscript Sources, 1745–1799.* 39 vols. Washington, DC: Government Printing Office, 1931–44.

WTJ   A. A. Lipscomb and A. E. Bergh, eds. *The Writings of Thomas Jefferson.* 20 vols. Washington, DC: Thomas Jefferson Memorial Association, 1900–1904.

1. Planning for Peace

1. George Washington, "To the New York Legislature," 26 June 1775, *WGW,* 3:305.

2. "The address and petition of the officers of the army of the United States," 29 Apr. 1783, *JCC,* 24:291.

3. For example, Madison wrote that the officers' petition would

"furnish new topics in favor the Impost." James Madison to Edmund Randolph, 30 Dec. 1782, *PJM,* 5:473.

4. Gouverneur Morris to John Jay, 1 Jan. 1783, in *The Life of Gouverneur Morris, with Selections from His Correspondence,* by Jared Sparks, vol. 1 (Boston: Gray & Bowen, 1832), 249.

5. Alexander McDougall to Henry Knox, 9 Jan. 1783, in *Letters of Members of the Continental Congress,* ed. Edmund Cody Burnett, vol. 7 (Washington, DC: Government Printing Office, 1934), 14.

6. Morris to Knox, 7 Feb. 1783, in ibid., 32n.

7. Alexander Hamilton to George Washington, 13 Feb. 1783, *PAH,* 3:254.

8. Ron Chernow, the biographer of Washington and Hamilton, wrote about the incident: "In suggesting that Washington exploit the situation to influence Congress, Hamilton toyed with combustible chemicals." Ron Chernow, *Washington: A Life* (New York: Penguin, 2010), 433. At the same time and probably in league with Hamilton, Gouverneur Morris sent a similar letter to Nathanael Greene, the leader of American forces in the South, suggesting that the army would only be paid if it united in demanding it. Richard Brookhiser, *Gentleman Revolutionary: Gouverneur Morris—The Rake Who Wrote the Constitution* (New York: Free Press, 2003), 72.

9. Washington to Hamilton, 4 Mar. 1783, *WGW,* 26:186–87.

10. Knox to McDougall, 21 Feb. 1783, Henry Knox Papers, 53:161, Massachusetts Historical Society.

11. Washington to Joseph Jones, 12 Mar. 1783, *WGW,* 26:214.

12. Along with Gates, Washington at first blamed Robert Morris but then shifted his accusation to Gouverneur Morris, who then served as Robert Morris's assistant. Compare Washington to Hamilton, 4 Apr. 1783, ibid., 26:293, with Washington to Hamilton, 16 Apr. 1783, ibid., 26:324. Stewart carried letters from Robert and Gouverneur Morris. See, generally, Charles Rappleye, *Robert Morris: Financier of the Revolution* (New York: Simon & Schuster, 2010), 331–51; and Richard H. Kohn, "The Inside History of the Newburgh Conspiracy," *William and Mary Quarterly,* 3rd ser., 27 (1970): 205–6.

13. James Madison, "Notes of Debates," 20 Feb. 1783, *JCC,* 25:906. See, generally, John Ferling, *The Assent of George Washington* (New York: Bloomsbury, 2009), 231–33; and William M. Fowler Jr., *Ameri-*

can Crisis: George Washington and the Dangerous Two Years after York-town, 1781–1783 (New York: Walker, 2011), 174–88. I also benefited from the insights freely and generously shared with me by James Kirby Martin, who was researching the Newburgh Conspiracy at Mount Vernon's Presidential Library for the Study of George Washington at the same time that I was working there on this book, but whose finished work has not yet been published.

14. [John Armstrong], address, 10 Mar. 1783, *JCC,* 24:295–97.

15. "General Orders," 11 Mar. 1783, *WGW,* 26:208.

16. [Armstrong], address, 12 Mar. 1783, *JCC,* 24:299.

17. Joseph J. Ellis, *His Excellency: George Washington* (New York: Knopf, 2004), 142.

18. George Washington, "To the Officers of the Army," 15 Mar. 1783, *WGW,* 26:226–27.

19. Ibid., 26:222n38.

20. Horatio Gates, minutes of meeting of officers, 15 Mar. 1783, *JCC,* 24:311.

21. George Washington, "Sentiments on a Peace Establishment," [May 1783], *WGW,* 26:374–98.

22. George Washington, "Circular to the States," 8 June 1783, ibid., 26:483–96.

23. Ibid.

24. Ibid.

25. James Thomas Flexner, *George Washington in the American Revolution* (Boston: Little, Brown, 1967), 514.

26. George Washington, "Farewell Orders to the Armies of the United States," 2 Nov. 1783, *WGW,* 27:224–27.

27. "December 10," *Massachusetts Spy,* 18 Dec. 1783, 3 (text of Washington's toast).

28. "Report of a Committee of Arrangements for the Public Audience," 22 Dec. 1783, *PTJ,* 6:410n1.

29. George Washington, address to Congress, 23 Dec. 1783, *JCC,* 25:837–38.

30. James McHenry to Margaret Caldwell, 23 Dec. 1783, *PTJ,* 6:406.

31. Thomas Mifflin, "Answer," 23 Dec. 1783, *JCC,* 25:838.

32. Ibid., 25:839.

33. Thomas Fleming, *The Perils of Peace* (New York: Collins, 2007),

33. The historian Joseph Ellis grandly concluded, "It was the greatest exit in American history." Ellis, *His Excellency,* 146.

34. Benjamin West, quoted in Garry Wills, *Cincinnatus: George Washington and the Enlightenment* (Garden City, NY: Doubleday, 1984), 13.

35. Jonathan Trumbull Jr., quoted in ibid.

36. See, e.g., "Extract of a Letter from a Gentleman in Annapolis," *New Jersey Gazette,* 6 Jan. 1784, 3.

37. McHenry to Caldwell, *PTJ,* 6:406.

38. Thomas Jefferson to Washington, 16 Apr. 1784, ibid., 7:106–7.

2. Empire Rising in the West

1. George Washington to Armand Louis de Gontaut, duc de Lauzun, 1 Feb. 1784, *PGW, CS,* 1:91.

2. Washington to Charles Bennett, 4th Earl of Tankerville, 20 Jan. 1784, ibid., 1:65.

3. Washington to Fielding Lewis Jr., 27 Feb. 1784, ibid., 1:161.

4. Washington to Tobias Lear, 31 July 1797, *PGW, RS,* 4:157.

5. In the only know exception to this rule, Washington remarked in his diary on June 30, 1785, that he had "dined with only Mrs. Washington, which I believe is the first instance of it since my retirement from public life." *GWD,* 30 June 1785, 2:386.

6. Washington to Jonathan Trumbull Jr., 5 Jan. 1784, *PGW, CS,* 1:12; Washington to Benjamin Harrison, 18 Jan. 1784, ibid., 1:57.

7. For a typical use by Washington of this phrase during the post-war period with reference to the frontier, see Washington to Chevalier de Chastellux, 12 Oct. 1783, *WGW,* 27:190.

8. See, e.g., Washington to Thomas Jefferson, 29 Mar. 1784, ibid., 27:374–76 (discussing their shared interest in giving priority to the public). In this respect, the historian W. W. Abbot noted, "From start to finish, Washington's interest in his country's advancing frontier was both personal and political. Private interest and public advantage were for him seldom at odds as he extended or developed his holding in the West." W. W. Abbot, "George Washington, the West, and the Union," in *George Washington Reconsidered,* ed. Don Higginbotham (Charlottesville: University of Virginia Press, 2001), 119.

9. *GWD,* 12 Sept. 1784, 2:288.

10. George Washington to Lund Washington, 20 Aug. 1775, *PGW, RWS,* 1:335.

11. *GWD,* 22 Sept. 1784, 2:297.

12. Washington to Jacob Read, 3 Nov. 1784, *PGW, CS,* 2:118–19.

13. *GWD,* 12 Sept. 1784, 2:290.

14. Washington to Henry Knox, 5 Dec. 1784, *PGW, CS,* 2:171.

15. Washington to George Plater, 25 Oct. 1784, *WGW,* 27:483.

16. Washington to Harrison, 10 Oct. 1784, *PGW, CS,* 2:92.

17. Washington to Richard Henry Lee, 18 June 1786, ibid., 4:118.

18. Washington to Read, ibid., 2:121.

19. Washington to Plater, *WGW,* 27:483.

20. *GWD,* 25 Sept. 1784, 2:307.

21. Ibid., 2:306.

22. Ibid., 2:306–7.

23. Ibid., 4 Oct. 1784, 2:317–18, 325.

24. "Editorial Note," *PGW, CS,* 2:86.

25. Washington to Harrison, 10 Oct. 1784, ibid., 2:92.

26. James Madison to Jefferson, 9 Jan. 1785, *PJM,* 8:228.

27. Washington to Gilbert du Motier, marquis de Lafayette, 15 Feb. 1785, *PGW, CS,* 2:366.

28. Washington to Lafayette, 25 July 1785, ibid., 3:152.

29. Washington to Benjamin Franklin, 26 Sept. 1785, ibid., 3:275.

30. *GWD,* 22 Sept. 1785, 2:415.

31. Washington to Madison, 30 Nov. 1785, *PGW, CS,* 3:420.

32. See, generally, Madison to Jefferson, *PJM,* 8:222–34.

3. Founding Federalism

1. John Jay to George Washington, 16 Mar. 1786, *PGW, CS,* 3:601.

2. Ibid., 3:602.

3. Washington to Jay, 18 May 1786, ibid., 4:55.

4. Ibid., 4:56.

5. Washington to Henry Knox, 26 Dec. 1786, ibid., 4:481.

6. Washington to James Madison, 5 Nov. 1786, ibid., 4:331.

7. Washington to Gilbert du Motier, marquis de Lafayette, 25 Mar. 1787, ibid., 5:106.

8. Washington to Madison, 31 Mar. 1787, ibid., 5:115–16.

9. See, e.g., Joseph J. Ellis, *The Quartet: Orchestrating the Second American Revolution, 1787–1788* (New York: Knopf, 2015), xiii.

10. George Washington, "Notes on the Sentiments on the Government of John Jay, Henry Knox, and James Madison," Apr. 1787, *PGW, CS,* 5:163–66.

11. Madison to Washington, 16 Apr. 1787, *PJM,* 9:383.

12. Madison to Edmund Pendleton, 24 Feb. 1787, ibid., 9:294–95.

13. Madison to Washington, 16 Apr. 1787, ibid., 9:383–85. For an extended discussion of Madison's views at this time on the subordination of the states to the national government, including the conception that they persist as corporations with delegated authority, see Mary Sarah Bilder, *Madison's Hand: Revising the Constitutional Convention* (Cambridge, MA: Harvard University Press, 2015), 43–44, 77, 98–100, 113.

14. Washington to Jay, 10 Mar. 1787, *PGW, CS,* 5:79–80; Washington to Knox, 3 Feb. 1787, ibid., 5:9; Washington to Madison, 31 Mar. 1787, ibid., 5:115–16.

15. Knox to Washington, 19 Apr. 1787, ibid., 5:96.

16. "Richmond, April 11," *Connecticut Journal,* 2 May 1787, 3.

17. "On the Coming of the American Fabius to the Federal Convention," *Providence (RI) Gazette,* 5 May 1787, 3.

18. "Philadelphia, May 11," *Maryland Chronicle,* 30 May 1787, 2.

19. Z, "For the Freeman's Journal," *Freeman's Journal,* 16 May 1787, 3.

20. Harrington, "For the Independent Gazetteer," *Independent Gazetteer,* 30 May 1787, 2.

21. George Mason to George Mason Jr., 18 May 1787, *PGM,* 3:880.

22. Votes at the Convention were recorded by state rather than by delegate, so in most cases it is not possible to determine how or whether individual delegates voted on various motions and resolutions. In his detailed analysis of Washington's role at the convention, the political scientist Glenn A. Phelps concluded that Washington "very likely voted on every substantive issue before the convention." Phelps, *George Washington and American Constitutionalism* (Lawrence: University of Kansas Press, 1993), 102.

23. For example, beyond his public advocacy of it prior to the convention, Washington's support for giving broad taxing authority to the general government was evident in his vote at the convention

against a ban on taxing exports. Over the objections of Madison and other big-state nationalists, the ban passed, with Virginia joining other export-rich plantation states in supporting it. Within the five-member Virginia delegation, however, Washington joined Madison in voting against it. Farrand, 21 Aug. 1787, 2:364.

24. Ibid., 29 May 1787, 1:18.

25. Ibid., 1:18–27 (notes of Madison, Robert Yates, and William Paterson).

26. Ibid., 1:23.

27. Washington to Thomas Jefferson, 30 May 1787, *PGW, CS,* 5:208.

28. Washington to David Stuart, 1 July 1787, ibid., 5:240. Stuart was the second husband of Washington's stepson's widow and a member of the Virginia House of Delegates.

29. Washington to Alexander Hamilton, 10 July 1787, ibid., 5:257.

30. Ferrand, 18–19 June 1787, 1:287–88, 323.

31. Washington to Lafayette, 15 Aug. 1787, *PGW, CS,* 5:296.

32. See, e.g., Paul Finkelman, "Slavery and the Constitutional Convention: Making a Covenant with Death," in *Beyond Confederation: Origins of the Constitution and American National Identity,* ed. Richard Beeman, Edward C. Carter II, and Stephen Botein (Chapel Hill: University of North Carolina, 1987), 221.

33. Pierce Butler to Weedon Butler, 5 May 1788, Farrand, 3:302.

34. See Max Farrand, *The Fathers of the Constitution: A Chronicle of the Establishment of the Union* (New Haven, CT: Yale University Press, 1921), 111 ("Washington was the great man of this day and the members not only respected and admired him; some of them were actually afraid of him").

35. Farrand, 1 June 1787, 1:65.

36. Ibid., 4 June 1787, 1:103.

37. Ibid., 1 June 1787, 1:66, and 2 June 1787, 1:88.

38. Ibid., 4 June 1787, 1:113. Randolph agreed that the three members of the executive should represent different sections of the country. Ibid., 2 June 1787, 1:65–66.

39. Ibid., 1 June 1787, 1:65–66, 70, 73. Making a similar comment, Rutledge at this point added, "A single man would feel the greatest responsibility and administer the public affairs best." Ibid., 1:65.

40. Ibid., 4 June 1787, 1:97.

41. Pierce Butler to Weedon Butler, in ibid., 3:302.

42. Farrand, 4 June 1787, 1:97.

43. United States Constitution, Art. II, sec. 2.

44. Letter to Congress, 17 Sept. 1787, in Farrand, 2:666–67, emphasis added (Morris's draft at ibid., 12 Sept. 1787, 2:583–84); resolutions of the convention, 17 Sept. 1787, in ibid., 2:665–66, emphasis added (committee draft at ibid., 13 Sept. 1787, 2:604–5).

45. Farrand, 17 Sept. 1787, 2:642.

46. Ibid., 2:648.

47. *GWD,* 17 Sept. 1787, 3:237.

48. Washington to Lafayette, 7 Feb. 1788, *PGW, CS,* 6:95.

4. Launching a Nation

1. George Washington to Gilbert du Motier, marquis de Lafayette, 18 Sept. 1787, *PGW, CS,* 5:334.

2. Quoted from Washington to Benjamin Harrison, 24 Sept. 1787, ibid., 5:339. In this letter to Harrison, Washington wrote that "the political concerns of this Country are, in a manner, suspended by a thread" and that if the convention had not agreed on the Constitution, "anarchy would soon have ensued." Ibid. Washington sent the same letter to former governors Benjamin Harrison, Patrick Henry, and Thomas Nelson. Ibid., 5:240.

3. In October Washington wrote, "It is highly probable that the refusal of our Governor and Colo. Mason to subscribe to the proceedings of the Convention will have a bad effect in this state." Washington to Henry Knox, 15 Oct. 1788, ibid., 5:376.

4. "To the Freemen of Pennsylvania," *Pennsylvania Gazette,* 10 Oct. 1787, 2, reprinted in *Independent Gazetter,* 15 Oct. 1787, 2.

5. In a private paper on the prospects for ratification probably dating from late September, Hamilton wrote at the outset, "The new constitution has in favour of its success . . . a very great weight of influence of the person who framed it, particularly in the universal popularity of General Washington." Alexander Hamilton, "Conjectures About the Constitution," Sept. 1787, *DHRC,* 13:277.

6. Gouverneur Morris to Washington, 30 Oct. 1787, *PGW, CS,* 5:400.

7. Hamilton, "Conjectures."

8. "Pennsylvania Gazette, 26 September," *DHRC,* 13:253 (notes to this DHRC entry indicate that the observation was reprinted in thirty-eight newspapers within three weeks).

9. For example, the principal French diplomat in the United States reported to his government in October that Americans "already speak of Gnl. Washington as the only man capable of filling the important position of President." Lois Guillaume Otto to Comte de Montmorin, 20 Oct. 1787, ibid., 13:423.

10. David Humphreys to Washington, 28 Sept. 1787, *PGW, CS,* 5:343.

11. Morris to Washington, 30 Oct. 1787, ibid., 5:400.

12. Washington to Humphreys, 10 Oct. 1787, ibid., 5:366.

13. George Washington to Bushrod Washington, 9 Nov. 1787, ibid., 5:421. In other letters from this period, Washington (like Morris) attributed much of the opposition to the Constitution to "sinister and self-important considerations" of opponents who would be adversely "affected by the change" in government. Washington to Humphreys, 10 Oct. 1787, ibid., 5:365; Washington to Knox, 15 Oct. 1787, ibid., 5:375.

14. Washington to James Madison, 10 Oct. 1787, ibid., 5:367. Regarding his close study of opposition arguments, see Washington to Alexander Hamilton, 28 Aug. 1788, ibid., 6:481.

15. Washington to Benjamin Lincoln, 2 Apr. 1788, ibid., 6:188. Washington believed that most people acted out of self-interest most of the time. See Edmund S. Morgan, "George Washington: The Aloof American," in *George Washington Reconsidered,* ed. Don Higginbotham (Charlottesville: University of Virginia Press, 2001), 289–91, 294–302.

16. Washington to John Armstrong, 25 Apr. 1788, *PGW, CS,* 6:226.

17. Alexander Donald to Thomas Jefferson, 12 Nov. 1787, *DHFFE,* 4:21–22.

18. Washington to Humphreys, 10 Oct. 1787, *PGW, CS,* 5:366. For examples of Washington distributing federalist literature, see Washington to David Stuart, 17 Oct. 1787, ibid., 5:379; and Washington to Stuart, 30 Nov. 1787, ibid., 5:467.

19. Madison to Washington, 20 Dec. 1787, ibid., 5:499.

20. Washington to Madison, 10 Jan. 1788, ibid., 6:33.

21. The first report appeared in "Carlisle, January 2," *Carlisle Ga-*

zette, 2 Jan. 1788, 3. It was reprinted eight days later in a newspaper that Washington generally read, the *Pennsylvania Packet,* and subsequently appeared in more than three dozen newspapers from New Hampshire to Georgia.

22. Washington to Lincoln, 31 Jan. 1788, *PGW, CS,* 6:74.

23. "Extracts of a Letter," *Massachusetts Gazette,* 25 Jan. 1788, 3. For the original letter, see Washington to Charles Carter, 14 Dec. 1787, *PGW, CS,* 5:489–92.

24. "Extracts of a Letter," 3.

25. "By Last Night's Mail," *Massachusetts Gazette,* 19 Oct. 1787, 2.

26. Washington to Lafayette, 28 May 1788, *PGW, CS,* 6:297.

27. Washington to Madison, 2 Mar. 1788, ibid., 6:137.

28. Washington to Lafayette, 28 Apr. 1788, ibid., 6:243.

29. Washington to Lincoln, 2 Apr. 1788, ibid., 6:188.

30. James Thomas Flexner, *George Washington and the New Nation* (Boston: Little, Brown, 1970), 150.

31. William Grayson, in "The Virginia Convention, Thursday, 24 June 1788," *DHRC,* 10:1498.

32. Washington to Charles Cotesworth Pinckney, 28 June 1788, *PGW, CS,* 6:361.

33. See, e.g., "The Tenth Pillar," *Maryland Journal,* 1 July 1788, *DHRC,* 10:1719 (reports on the celebration in Baltimore, where "the illustrious George Washington" received the third toast, after toasts to the Constitution and the last two states to ratify, Virginia and New Hampshire).

34. James Monroe to Jefferson, 12 July 1788, ibid., 10:1705.

35. Washington to Edward Newenham, 29 Aug. 1788, *PGW, CS,* 6:387–88.

36. Washington to Lafayette, 18 June 1788, ibid., 6:338.

37. In a late-June letter to Washington, written after the Virginia convention, Madison depicted the antifederalists' new strategy as getting "a Congress appointed in the first instance that will commit suicide on their own Authority." Madison to Washington, 27 June 1788, ibid., 6:356.

38. Washington to Madison, 23 Sept. 1788, ibid., 6:534.

39. Washington to Lincoln, 28 Aug. 1788, ibid., 6:483. For similar comments by Washington, see Washington to James McHenry, 31

July 1788, ibid., 6:409–10, and Washington to Madison, 23 Sept. 1788, ibid., 6:534.

40. Washington to Madison, 23 Sept. 1788, ibid., 6:534.

41. *Maryland Journal,* 13 Jan. 1789, *DHFFE,* 2:199–200.

42. Washington to Samuel Powel, 5 Feb. 1789, *PGW, PS,* 1:281.

43. Hamilton to Washington, 18 Nov. 1788, ibid., 1:119.

44. Morris to Washington, 6 Dec. 1788, ibid., 1:165.

45. Lincoln to Washington, 24 Sept. 1788, ibid., 1:8.

46. Morris to Washington, 30 Oct. 1787, *PGW, CS,* 5:400.

47. See, e.g., Washington to Benjamin Fishbourn, 23 Dec. 1788, *PGW, PS,* 1:199.

48. Washington to William Pierce, 1 Jan. 1789, *WGW,* 30:175.

49. Morris to Washington, 6 Dec. 1788, *PGW, PS,* 1:166.

50. Reporting to Lincoln on Virginia's ratification of the Constitution, Washington wrote of his joy at every step taken by Americans "to render the Nation happy at home & respected abroad." Washington to Lincoln, 29 June 1788, *PGW, CS,* 6:365.

51. Washington to Richard Henderson, 19 June 1788, ibid., 6:340.

52. Commenting on his state's electors, the Virginia federalist Henry Lee reassured a doubtful Washington, who thought that antifederalists might oppose his election to weaken the new government, "Among the electors will be many antifederal characters, but not one of them will act on the principles you suggest in their choice of president." Henry Lee to Washington, 17 Jan. 1789, *PGW, PS,* 1:247–48. See also "Philadelphia, 6th January," *Federal Gazette,* 6 Jan. 1789, 3 ("We hear from Virginia, that the anti-federalists intend to vote for General Washington, as president, but that Governor Clinton will have all their votes for vice-president of the United States"). For Clinton's support for Washington's election as president, see George Clinton to Washington, 10 Mar. 1789, *PGW, PS,* 1:378; and John P. Kaminski, *George Clinton: Yeoman Politician of the New Republic* (Madison, WI: Madison House, 1993), 172.

53. See, e.g., Kenneth R. Bowling, "George Washington's Vision for the United States," in "The Vision of the Founders," ed. Peter Onuf and Robert McDonald (unpublished manuscript) ("It belongs with the 1783 Address to the States and the 1786 Farewell Address as the most extensive and detailed statements of Washington's political

views"); Flexner, *New Nation,* 162–64 ("Even in its mutilated form, the discarded inaugural is an extremely important document").

54. "Fragments of a Draft of the First Inaugural Address," Jan. 1789, in *George Washington: Writings,* ed. John Rhodehamel (New York: Library of America, 1997), 706–9.

55. Ibid., 707–9, 712, 715–16.

56. "Address by Charles Thomson," 14 Apr. 1789, *PGW, PS,* 2:54–55. Thomson also delivered a formal letter from the Senate president pro tem, John Langdon, informing Washington of the vote and expressing Langdon's hope "that so auspicious a mark of public confidence will meet your approbation." John Langdon to Washington, 6 Apr. 1789, ibid., 2:29.

57. "Address to Charles Thomson," 14 Apr. 1789, ibid., 2:56. Washington also gave Thomson a formal letter for Langdon in which he declared his decision "to obey the important & flattering call of my Country." Washington to Langdon, 14 Apr. 1789, ibid., 2:54.

58. Because Washington's diary for the trip is lost, no record exists of the servants who accompanied this trip other than a letter from Tobias Lear noting that Washington's longtime, favorite valet, William Lee, went along as far as Philadelphia, where he reinjured his knee and was forced to remain for medical treatment. Lear's letter also suggests that the Mount Vernon coachman Jacob Jacobus, an indentured servant, served as a driver. Tobias Lear to George Augustine Washington, 3 May 1789, unpublished letter, First Federal Congress Project (copy supplied by project coeditor Kenneth R. Bowling). Typically, Washington would travel on such a journey with a rider on the front horse, a driver on an outside front seat, and a valet on an outside rear seat.

5. The Coronation

1. *DGW,* 16 Apr. 1789, 5:445.

2. "To George Washington, Esquire" and "His Excellency's Answer," *Gazette of the United States,* 29 Apr. 1789, 24.

3. "Baltimore, April 21," *Pennsylvania Packet,* 28 Apr. 1789, 2.

4. "Address of the Citizens of Baltimore," *Federal Gazette,* 27 Apr. 1789, 2.

5. The ode is dated April 16, 1789, Bladensburg, Maryland, which

was the nearest town to Spurrier's Tavern, but it was first published in a Baltimore newspaper. "From the Maryland Journal," *Pennsylvania Packet,* 1 May 1789, 3.

6. "Wilmington, April 25," ibid., 28 Apr. 1789, 3. For an account of Washington's route and stops, see Mary V. Thompson, "Historical Background on George Washington's First Inauguration," unpublished Mount Vernon background paper, 21 May 2015, 4.

7. Accounts differ on whether the wreath landed on Washington's head or was suspended above it, though one contemporary article clearly states that the wreath fell "within a short distance of the Excellency's head as he passed under it." "Philadelphia, April 21," *Independent Gazetteer,* 21 Apr. 1789, 3. Peale family accounts have Washington brushing off the wreath but kissing Angelica. James Thomas Flexner, *George Washington and the New Nation* (Boston: Little, Brown, 1970), 175, also states that that wreath "landed on his head."

8. "Philadelphia, 20 April," *Federal Gazette,* 20 Apr. 1789, 2; "Philadelphia, April 29," *Freemans's Journal,* 29 Apr. 1789, 3; "Philadelphia, 22 April," *New-York Daily Gazette,* 27 Apr. 1789, 410; William Spohn Baker, *Washington After the Revolution* (Philadelphia: Lippincott, 1898), 124, containing the text of the article from the *Pennsylvania Gazette.*

9. "Philadelphia, 21 April," *Federal Gazette,* 21 Apr. 1789, 3.

10. "Philadelphia, 22 April," ibid., 22 Apr. 1789, 3. Morris was not at home for Washington's 1789 visit because he had already taken his seat in the federal Senate.

11. "Trenton, April 21, 1789," *Gazette of the United States,* 25 Apr. 1789, 19.

12. "Trenton," *New-York Daily Gazette,* 1 May 1789, 426.

13. "A Sonata," *Federal Gazette,* 25 Apr. 1789, 3.

14. "Philadelphia, May 1," *Philadelphia Packet,* 1 May 1789, 2. Following the serenade, Washington wrote a note of appreciation to the singers stating (in the third person) that the event "made such impressions on his remembrance, as, he assures them, will never be effaced." George Washington to the Ladies of Trenton, 21 Apr. 1789, *PGW, PS,* 2:108.

15. "New-Brunswick, April 7," *Pennsylvania Packet,* 13 Apr. 1789, 3.

16. "In our account," *New-York Packet,* 1 May 1789, 3.

17. "Ode to be Sung on the Arrival of the President of the United

States," *New-York Daily Gazette,* 23 Apr. 1789, 398. Several sources note that this song was sung by a mixed chorus on the boat.

18. Elias Boudinot to Hannah Boudinot, 24 Apr. 1789, in *The History of the Centennial Celebration of the Inauguration of George Washington,* ed. Clarence Winthrop Bowen (New York: Appleton, 1892), 29.

19. "New York, April 25," *Gazette of the United States,* 25 Apr. 1789, 15.

20. "Diary of William Maclay," 24 Apr. 1789 and 8 May 1789, *DHFFC,* 9:4–5, 28–29; James H. Hutson, "John Adams' Title Campaign," *New England Quarterly* 41 (1968): 31–34. The text of Adams's speech was not recorded. His proposed titles appear in private letters, but at least one senator noted that Adams also suggested titles in the Senate. "Diary of William Maclay," 8 May 1789, 28. At the time, the vice president, as the presiding officer of the Senate, could both speak and propose motions in the Senate. The Senate revoked these privileges in part due to Adams's abuse of them. In a letter to Washington, Adams wrote about the presidency, "Neither Dignity, nor Authority, can be Supported in human Minds collected into nations or any great numbers without a Splendor and Majisty, in Some degree, proportioned to them." John Adams to Washington, 17 May 1789, *PGW, PS,* 2:314.

21. *Annals of Congress,* 23 Apr. 1789, 1:24 (Senate).

22. "Diary of William Maclay," 24 Apr. 1789, 4.

23. Ibid., 8 May 1789, 28–29.

24. *Annals of Congress,* 25 Apr. 1789, 1:25 (Senate).

25. "New-York, May 1," *New-York Daily Gazette,* 1 May 1789, 426, emphasis added. For the shift in venue, see *Annals of Congress,* 27 Apr. 1789, 1:25 (Senate).

26. *Annals of Congress,* 29 Apr. 1789, 1:241 (House).

27. See, e.g., from Washington's time in New York, R—— R—— to S——, 1 May 1789, "Notes and Queries," *Historical Magazine* 3 (1859): 184 ("I caught his eye, and had the honor of a very gracious bow from him: this, from so great a man in so high a station, I thought myself highly honored").

28. Thomas Jefferson, *The Anas, WTJ,* 1:279–80.

29. "Fragments of a Draft of the First Inaugural Address," Jan. 1789, in *George Washington: Writings,* ed. John Rhodehamel (New York: Library of America, 1997), 707. He went on to observe in the

address that "whenever a government is to be instituted or changed by Consent of the people, confidence in the person placed at the head of it, is, perhaps, more peculiarly necessary."

30. See Washington to David Stuart, 26 July 1789, *PGW, PS,* 3:322.

31. At the outset, the New York chancellor, Robert Livingston, advised as much when Washington asked for his views on the etiquette proper for the president. That titles, formality, and restricted access are "not essentially necessary I infer from the unlimited respect which every rank of Citizen feels for our Excellency tho in your public life you indulged them in an easy access," Livingston wrote to Washington. "Hereditary Monarchs must in the common course of things be frequently men of little abilities & often have great defects, it is therefore necessary to surround them with guards & to dazel beholders with a false glare. Elective Magistrates are known before they are elected, their virtues are the cause of their elevation, the exposing these to [the] public can not tend to diminish the respect which they originally created." Robert R. Livingston to Washington, 2 May 1789, ibid., 2:193–94.

32. Flexner, *New Nation,* 193.

33. *DGW,* 23 Apr. 1789, 5:447.

34. Washington to Edward Rutledge, 5 May 1789, *PGW, PS,* 2:217.

35. Adams to Benjamin Rush, 19 Mar. 1812, in *The Spur of Fame: Dialogues of John Adams and Benjamin Rush, 1805–1813,* ed. John A. Schultz and Douglas Adair (San Marino, CA: Huntington, 1966), 211–12. In a similar vein, Adams famously commented on Washington's style that "Virginian Geese are all Swans" and appraised it as worth "five Talents." Adams to Rush, 11 Nov. 1807, in *Old Family Letters,* ed. Alexander Biddle (Philadelphia: Lippincott, 1892), 169.

36. Washington to Stuart, *PGW, PS,* 3:323.

37. About this dining arrangement, Lear wrote at the time, "We have engaged Black Sam Frances [*sic*] as Steward & superintendent of the Kitchen, and a very excellent fellow he is in that latter department— he tosses up such a number of fine dishes that we are distracted in our choice when we set down to table, and obliged to hold a long consultation upon the subject before we can determine what to attack." Tobias Lear to George Augustine Washington, 3 May 1789, unpublished letter, First Federal Congress Project (copy supplied by project coeditor

Kenneth R. Bowling). Probably of mixed French and African descent, Samuel Fraunces, known as "Black Sam," was born in the Caribbean and had moved to New York by 1755. He had opened what became known as Fraunces Tavern in 1762. Washington had held the farewell dinner with his officers at the tavern on December 4, 1783. During his first week in New York, in addition to hiring Fraunces, Washington added two liveried footmen, a porter, and a maid to the staff he had brought from Mount Vernon. Ultimately, Washington's household staff in New York numbered about twenty and included a mix of paid workers, slaves, and indentured servants.

38. Washington to Stuart, *PGW, PS,* 3:322. Lear also discussed this crush of midday visitors in Lear to George Augustine Washington, 3 May 1789, unpublished letter, First Federal Congress Project ("We have no company to eat or drink with us — but hitherto there has been the greatest abundance from 9 a.m. to 3 p.m. to pay their *etiquettical congee*").

39. The best direct evidence that Madison either drafted or assisted in drafting Washington's first inaugural address appears in a letter of 4 May from Washington asking Madison "to finish the good work" he had started by writing the president's reply to the House response to the inaugural address. Washington to Madison, 5 May 1789, *PGW, PS,* 2:216. Madison had also written the House response, so in writing Washington's reply he would be replying to his own response to his own address. Because of his dual role as House leader and key presidential adviser, the editors of the Madison Papers depict Madison as "in effect the 'prime minister'" during this period and attribute Washington's inaugural address to Madison. "Editorial Note," *PJM,* 12:120–21.

40. "Of To-Morrow," *Gazette of the United States,* 29 Apr. 1789, 19.

41. Washington Irving, *Life of George Washington* (New York: Putnam's Sons, 1882), 581. Born in 1783, Irving was named for George Washington, who, when told that, reportedly patted the youngster's head. Contemporary accounts vary somewhat on the order of the procession, with some putting the heads of the departments in front of Washington and some noting that the diplomatic corps rode among the invited dignitaries. The order presented in the text appeared in many newspapers.

42. "Diary of William Maclay," 30 Apr. 1789, 11–12.

43. No precise estimate of the number of spectators survives. Some accounts refer to thousands, while several local newspapers simply call it "an immense concourse of citizens." See, e.g. "New-York, May 7," *New-York Journal,* 7 May 1789, 3.

44. Eliza Susan Quincy, *Memoir of the Life of Eliza S. M. Quincy* (Boston: Wilson & Son, 1861), 51. The author used her maiden name, Morton, at the time of the inauguration.

45. Ibid., 51–52.

46. *Annals of Congress,* 30 Apr. 1789, 1:27 (Senate).

47. Joseph J. Ellis, *His Excellency: George Washington* (New York: Knopf, 2004), 186.

48. Adams to Rush, 11 Nov. 1807, in Biddle, *Old Family Letters*, 170.

49. Diego de Gardoqui to Florida Blanca, 1 May 1789, in Bowen, *History of the Centennial Celebration,* 49. Maclay used the word "ungainly" in his account, but others made similar observations. "Diary of William Maclay," 30 Apr. 1789, 13.

50. *Annals of Congress,* 30 Apr. 1789, 1:27–29 (Senate). In speaking about God in this formal address, Washington never actually spoke the word *God*. Instead, he referred to "the Great Author of every public and private good" at one point and "the benign Parent of the human race" at another.

51. Although many accounts only mention Washington visiting Livingston's mansion to view the fireworks, Lear (who was with him) noted that he also stopped at the nearby home of Henry Knox, "where we had a full view of the works." Lear to George Augustine Washington, 3 May 1789, unpublished letter, First Federal Congress Project.

52. Ibid.

53. "New-York, May 1," *Daily Advertiser,* 1 May 1789, 2.

54. Gouverneur Morris to Washington, 30 Oct. 1787, *PGW, CS,* 5:400.

55. "Farewell Address," 19 Sept. 1796, in Rhodehamel, *George Washington: Writings,* 965. Original printed versions in newspapers of the day set the word *American* in capital letters, the only word so emphasized in the document.